THE MUTINIES AND THE PEOPLE

OR

STATEMENTS OF NATIVE FIDELITY

THE MUTINIES AND THE PEOPLE

OR

STATEMENTS OF NATIVE FIDELITY

EXHIBITED

DURING THE OUTBREAK OF 1857-58.

BY

SAMBHU CHANDRA MUKHERJEE
(A HINDU)

GYAN

Published by

Gyan Publishing House
5, Ansari Road
Daryaganj, New Delhi-110002
Phone: 011-47034999, 9811692060
E-mail: books@gyanbooks.com

Distribution Network
gyanbooks.com
India, USA, Canada, UK, Australia

ISBN: 978-81-212-5983- 5 (PB)
First Published, 1859

2nd Impression 2024

Printed at: Gyan Press, Delhi.

THE MUTINIES AND THE PEOPLE OR STATEMENTS OF NATIVE FIDELITY
Author: SAMBHU CHANDRA MUKHERJEE (A HINDU)

THE MUTINIES AND THE PEOPLE

OR

STATEMENTS OF

NATIVE FIDELITY

EXHIBITED

DURING THE OUTBREAK OF 1857-58.

BY

A HINDU.

CALCUTTA:

PUBLISHED BY THE "BANGABASI" OFFICE,

38-2, Bhawani Charan Dutt's Street.

1905.

INTRODUCTION.

—:o:—

There is a class of Englishmen here and at home who consider the British Empire in India as a miracle, without sufficiently recognising the significance of the word. It is certainly not a miracle in the Biblical sense of the word, but as the current acceptance of the word goes, the British Empire in India may be a miracle in so far as its origin and growth can not be accounted for by any process of common reasoning. We believe the origin of the British Rule in India lies more in oriental fidelity and gratitude than in the prowess of the British troops. When Englishmen appeared on the political arena of India in the capacity of traders, the country was acutely suffering from anarchy and taking advantage of the unsafe state of the country a batch of clever Englishmen built an Empire that looks now like a miracle. In this empire-building, the Englishmen were greatly helped by native statesmen and troops, and as long as the native feelings and sentiments were honoured by Englishmen, the Empire did not encounter any serious danger.

The Mutiny gave a rude shock to many Englishmen who believed in the fidelity of native troops. When the upheaval took place and the massacre of the Innocents occurred at Cawnpore a certain class of Englishmen cried aloud for punishing the infidelity of the native races forgetting that the rising was mainly due to the recklessness of some ardent English military men in forcing the sepoys to use greased cartridges. Lord Canning who was much abused at the time for his policy of clemency never paid heed to these reckless cries and believed that the rising could be quelled by taking into confidence the natives of the land.

This book was an opportune publication by an Indian Journalist to show to the Englishmen who cried for vengeance at the time, by quoting chapter and verse from official gazettes that the civil population never lagged in their fidelity to quell the great insurrection.

THE BANGABASI OFFICE,
Calcutta, July, 1905.

THE PUBLISHER.

NATIVE FIDELITY

DURING THE MUTINY.

CHAPTER I.

"NOTHING," says a writer on the Sepoy mutiny in the April number of the *Edinburgh Review*, "has been more remarkable than the fact that, throughout its whole progress it has faithfully retained the character of a military revolt. It has involved the whole Native Bengal army; it has spread to the Northern contingents; it has reached some Bombay regiments; it has touched the Nizam's army; it has threatened the Madras army, but except in the newly annexed State of Oude, it has not been taken up by the population.

Now it is this circumstance which has saved India to England. If, as at the Sicilian Vespers, the whole population of India, with its tens of millions, had at the first signal of resistance, risen against the English, our rule in India might, perhaps, by great exertions and large expenditure, have been recovered, but we should only have recovered a population watching the next favorable opportunity for revolt and have re-established an empire on sand. It was the general good will of the population which rendered the suppression of the military mutiny both practicable and beneficial." (No. 218, 1858). And the London *Times*, which is universally esteemed as the exponent and leader of popular opinion in England, so early as July 1857, declared the same sentiment. It was the first English journal which spoke out upon the military character of the revolt and attributed the salvation of the Indian Empire as a dependency of Great Britain to the fidelity, aid, and advice of the people of the country during the insurrection.

"From all sides we are assured," said the *Times*, "that the general population has exhibited rather good will than hostility towards us, and in many cases effectual protection has been afforded to fugitives from Delhi (and other scenes of mutiny)." Nearly a year has elapsed since those words were written, and they have been signally verified by the events that have so quickly and crowdedly followed. The time was certainly most troublous and tempting, and how admirable must be the moral courage of those, who, while the mutiny of a whole army was becoming partially successful, and the vestiges of authority and order were being swept away from most of the provinces of Northern India, did not only observe a peaceful neutrality by standing unmoved amidst the tide of insurrectionary feeling which then overflooded Hindoostan proper, but also, at the risk of their property, lives and family-safety, proved such ready and effectual instruments of salvation to many utterly helpless European fugitives, and acted as protectors and conservators of order at so unruly and perilous an occasion. The struggle was a sore trial of the nation's fidelity.

It is difficult, if not impossible, to cite another instance in the history of a country, governed by a nation, foreign in language, in birth, blood and creed, of so remarkable an attachment and loyalty to its foreign rulers at such a crisis. This feature of the revolution which the Bengal soldiery has so ruthlessly attempted to force upon India, at once stamps the character of the insurrection as purely military. The acts of active Native fidelity, perform-ed under the greatest difficulties imaginable, so much so as in the very scenes of the revolt, under the eyes of the insurgents, and with bloody threats from them within the hearing of the actors, which it is intended to cite and embody in the following pages, will conclusively show that the feeling of revolt and disloyalty was not shared in by the mass of the people, even though the movement was headed by the House of Delhi and conducted by a body of soldiers whose bravery, discipline and skill had established British dominion from the Hymalayas to the Cape Comorin, and made the name of the Honorable E. I. Company respected and feared throughout the continent of Asia. But these instances are only a few among a host of those which have found entrance into the columns of contemporary journals, and which, the writer hopes, will one day be presented to the public as a supplement to the history of this memorable event, and a monument to the memory of those who performed the duties of subject, man and brother in the face of the most appalling dangers that surrounded them. Such a work would be most befitting the patriot or philanthropist who takes an interest in the cause of Indian loyalty and humanity. If any of our readers has taken notes of the passing events of the mutiny, he will not be at a loss to observe the finger of Providence working in the minds of the people, and to solve the important problem of England's salvation from this overwhelming deluge of Indian insurrection. We need only add that the instances which we quote below are those that were recorded by men who have, since the breaking out of the mutiny, displayed the most rancorous animosity to the people of this country and whose testimony therefore must be taken as a contribution to Truth which they could not refuse. There are no doubt many instances which have not got into print, but the value of which nevertheless stands as high as that of those noticed by publicists and news-writers. We should also mention that the facts of the kind herein recorded, are so scattered and extend over so large an area that we have scant opportunities to give them entire. We have not all the records before us for avail and we must content ourselves with what we have got. It is however hoped that the Commission of Enquiry into the causes of the mutiny for the appointment of which instructions from the Court of Directors have already arrived will not fail, as they will have the best means and greatest opportunities for this important work, to record the instances of Native fidelity and service that may come to their knowledge during the investigation, and when the period arrives for them to give the history of the revolt, they will chronicle the deeds which have warded off the dangers of a popular revolution from attending the military outbreak, and prevented the antagonism of the Sepoys from proving successful as a crusade of extermination against the Europeans in India.

CHAPTER II.

WHETHER this mutiny was a pre-concerted plan and had a previous deep organization, is yet an open question. The trial of the King of Lelhi which was expected to clear the doubts, has left the problem as far from solution as before. But one thing is certain. It has taken the Government and the country equally by surprise. Whatever may the prophets after the event, contend as to the presaged moral certainty of the outbreak, none can deny that when the storm came, nobody expected it, and both the European and Native populations were equally surprised to find themselves in the midst of a bloody rebellion.

This unexpected burst paralyzed the efforts of the native population in the vicinity of the outbreak, who, though willing to offer every aid in their power to the Europeans thus threatened and pursued, and anxious to protect the old land-marks of order, were completely restrained in their wishes from the fear of the Sepoys. We read in the papers so many instances of villagers foregoing the (to them) most welcome duties of hospitality from an absolute dread of the mutineers, but still secretly rendering all friendly aid possible, that we are tempted to ask whether the history of any nation under such difficulties, records such acts of pure benevolence and gratitude. Thus we find in Chambers' Historical Narrative of the Sepoy Revolt, repeated instances of this description, in which the villagers could do no lengthened acts of kindness from an overpowering fear of the insurgents. In a story of escape of four European fugitives from Delhi, it is stated that "they crept on the whole day, obtaining a little food and water from the villagers, who were however too much afraid to afford the fugitives the shelter of a roof." In another "kindness was accorded to them (the fugitives) for one whole day, after which the humane natives turned, lest the Sepoys should burn their village, if they heard of Feringees having been harboured, declared they could no longer afford shelter." Further, we perceive that the villagers, too much moved by the piteous condition of the same party, but scarcely able to show kindness openly, invited them to an "out-house containing twenty cows, the only roof that the owner dared to offer them." Another party, faint and hungered by a hot pursuit of a band of Sepoys, were eagerly searching for refuge when "a few Hindoo peasants, discovering them, told them where they could hide in a tope of trees, and brought them *chuphatees* (bread) and milk," unable by the ever-present dread of the Sepoys, to receive them into their homes. We could multiply such instances without number, but we shall not go to an unnecessary length; these are sufficient to convince the reader of the terrible check under which the first success of the Sepoys held the love of hospitality, common to the people of this country. It is true that among those who were distinguished for conspicuous acts of protection and fidelity, there were some who joined the rebels when the Sepoy cause was in the full tide of success, but we should remember that that was the only alternative left to them. They were, as the Noble Earl of Derby has well put it, seduced from their allegiance by the pressure of temptation, or compelled by the force of circumstances.

The mutiny commenced at Meerut, but Delhi was the focus and stronghold of the Sepoy disaffection. The following, which we quote from a letter published in the *Times*, written by an officer at Kurnal, describes the providential escape which that officer effected from Delhi, through the aid of the people of the neighbouring villages. Like every European who had the misfortune to dwell at that fatal time in the imperial city, he was unprepared for the struggle, but the love of life is too strong for man to conquer—and with his weak health he rushed forth to sell his blood as dearly as possible. Finding himself unequal to the contest he changed his policy and feigned death. This device succeeded and he was left for dead. We shall now leave him to tell in his own words the story of his salvation after this terrible episode in the history of his escape :—

"About one hour after I came to, and managed to stagger on about a mile without shoes, where I secreted myself in a hut until day-break, when I resumed my dreary journey, and, after travelling about twelve miles, the latter part of which was in the broiling sun without anything on my head, arrived at Alleepore. I managed to beg a little water, some bread, and a few old native clothes to cover my nakedness, but was refused shelter. Again I went on and on through the ploughed fields, barefooted, fearing to keep the road, on account of the robbers, and after being turned from mutinous villages, came to a village where the head man, much against the wishes of his labourers, offered to secrete me. This offer accepted, and I remained with him for five days, although I saw the Sirdars came there and wished to murder me, but seeing my helpless state and how ill I was, they refrained from doing so and went away; and a second time I was forced to flee to the fields and hide myself, as about 50 of the mutinous sepoys came and searched the village for Europeans, but after lying the whole day in the sun my generous friend the Zemindar came and sheltered me."—*Times, July 20th*, 1857.

This officer's wife and child, with a knot of friends, were protected by a Ranee Mungha Dabee.

A boy of 19, writing from Meerut, makes

mention of the following in an interesting story of his escape from Delhi :—

"It would be too long, my very dearest sister, to tell you of how for three days and nights we wandered in the jungles, sometimes fed and sometimes robbed by the villagers, till at length, wearied and footsore, with shreds of cloths on our backs we arrived at a village where they put us in a hut and fed us for four days, and moreover took a note from us into Meerut, whence an escort of cavalry was sent out, and we were brought safely in here."—*Times*, 22*nd July*.

CHAPTER III.

THE following just emarks and candid admissions of an experienced Anglo-Indian, deserve the particular attention of those who entertain any doubts as to the purely military character of the revolt and to the facts of protection and aid offered by the people, mostly under personal risks and difficulties, the appalling nature of which places their fidelity and the integrity of their intentions above suspicion. Many from whatever motives have averred that there is no gratitude in this land, but the invariable good conduct in hours of peril of native ryots, Ooryah bearers, and those villagers who owed the slightest benefit to the *Shaib-loges*, rescued by them as testified by the writer quoted below, and by others with the weight of national responsibility on their heads, such as Mr. Russel, the *Times's* Special Correspondent and Mr. Layard demonstratively proves to the contrary. With regard to the fidelity and attachment of the Zemindars, Mr. Mangles, the late Chairman of the Court of Directors, has well said that their universal good conduct forms a distinctive feature of this revolution. Indeed instances of their firmness and allegiance are so numerous that many well informed Indian thinkers whose minds had hitherto strongly been set against them, have come to the opinion that the best safeguard of the British Government against calamities of the kind which has so terribly convulsed it, lies in the extension of the far-seeing and most statesmanlike land settlement system of Lord Cornwallis. The reader will find in these pages ample instances of the active fidelity of this important class of British subjects recorded, not by contemporary journals only, but also by Government Secretaries and other officials of note.

But in spite of the authentic statements of these high authorities, there is a class of writers who maintain that the Natives of India are not susceptible of kindness, and that the worst way of governing them is that through their affections. Baron Macaulay, though not a little ungenerous to their national characteristics, does not still refuse to record that the attachment of the Sepoys to Clive, was almost child-like, and that there is not an instance in which kindness, however scantily exhibited towards the Natives, was not appreciated with the utmost readiness, and returned at the shortest opportunity with the greatest pleasure. But the best answer to these allegations is contained in a remark which we observe among other very enlightened and truthful sentiments teeming in one of the best written articles on India, in the last number of the *Westminster Review*, which we remember to have read for a long time since. Alluding to the treatment of the Natives, the writer says, "Forsooth, Orientals are so accustomed to be ill-treated that they will despise and regret if you treat them well; just so our grandfathers and great grandfathers used to speak of the Irish; it is the universal doctrine of the tyrant." As to the future policy of England towards India—whether it should be one governing the country through the affections of the people or ruling it on autocratic principles,—it is irrelevant to the subject-matter before us. But we may be allowed to observe that the wisdom of the British Parliament has decided upon a policy of governing India for its teeming millions, and through their good will and love, and no interested views of Indian rule, prompted by a race-antagonism, and race-hatred, if not by other sinister motives, can now avail.

The writer alluded to above says :—

"With the exception of the Goojurs, who are hereditary marauders, the Zemindars have behaved well to us, which is a great encouragement to good government, for there cannot be a doubt that it is mainly owing to the 30 years' settlement which has secured them against the unlimited exactions of the old revenue system. The uniform fidelity of the native domestic servants, both male and female, has also been very remarkable, and the instances have not been few in which they have protected their masters and mistresses at the hazard of their lives The poor *Ayas* have repeatedly carried off the infants intrusted to them amid a shower of balls. These things prove that the people are not insensible to just and kind treatment and indicate that there must have been something wrong in our management of the Sepoys, who in former days yielded to none in attachment to their English *Officers*."—*Times*, 22*nd July*, 1857.

The subjoined is an acknowledgment of the protection offered to the writer by the Rajah of Benares, on the occasion of the outbreak in that Jerusalem of India :—

"We did not take the direct road to Chunar on account of the mutineers who took that direction, but we crossed the river to Ramnuggur, a fort and palace belonging to the Rajah of Benares. There we bivouacked for the night. The Rajah himself, who was obliged to fly from Benares during the night, was very kind to us, and gave us provisions, &c. But, as he feared the responsibility of sheltering us, he sent us on with a guard of his Sepoys to Chunar."—*Times*, 5*th August*, 1857.

CHAPTER IV.

SADLY torn as the affections of the British people have been by the painful events of the mutiny, their feelings of indignation and revenge have been roused not against the mutineers only but against the whole Native population. We regret this inasmuch as it is unjust, unreasonable, and incompatible with the mission of England in India. But the language has been especially virulent against the Brahmins whose love of religious domination, it is said, led them to invent those absurd rumours of Government interference with the faiths of the people, which have occasioned these bloody horrors. What truth there is in this not unplausible charge, the solution of the causes of the revolt will disclose. But none can deny that if the Brahmins were more than reasonably zealous about their religion, still the history of their conduct during the insurrection, marks some of the most remarkable instances of humanity, hospitality, and, if we may use the expression, religiousness that have ever occurred. It was not the love of power, love of sovereignty, love of revenge or of extermination which actuated the Brahmin Sepoys, but of God and of their peculiar mode of His worship, which they thought, however unreasonably, Government intended to destroy. But as a demonstration of the religious character of their movement they have throughout conducted themselves with religious rigor and punctuality. They did not murder, as far as we have read, their officers or stain their hands with the blood of innocent women and children. On the contrary they earnestly entreated in many cases their officers to leave the regiment, and often communicated to them the state of feeling prevailing among the corps. Some time they interposed their authority for the protection of ladies and children, and not unfrequently exhorted their brethren to desist from the brutal acts of the sword and fire. Every body has read the opportune and eloquent speech which the lamented Sir Henry Lawrence addressed to the wavering regiments stationed at Luck now after the intelligence of the Delhi outbreak had arrived, which had the wholesome effect of settling turbulent spirits, though for a time only. In it he mentioned the names of four men whose exemplary loyalty he earnestly recommended to their unfortunate brethren. The first three of them were Brahmins and the good Chief thus spoke of them:—"Now turn to these good and faithful soldiers—Subadar Sewak Tewaree, Havildar Heralall Doobey, and Sephai Ramru·Doobey of the 48th Native Infantry, who have set to you all a good example. The first three at once arrested the bearer of a seditious letter and brought the whole circumstance to the notice of superior authority." To the common temptation the unfortunate 1st N. I., which was, at the date of the revolt, stationed at Cawnpore, yielded on the 5th June, 1857, and marched out of the lines at about three o'clock in the morning, but "before doing so (says the writer of Chambers' History of the Revolt in India), the Sepoys, (most of whom were Brahmins) showed a lingering affection for the English officers of the regiment; these officers had, for some time, been in the habit of sleeping in the quarter-guard of the regiment, to indicate their confidence in the men; and now the men begged—nay forced them to go into the intrenchment as a means of personal safety." When the disarmed 26th Regiment of Light Infantry mutinied at Mean Meer, "the Havildar, Major, and Pay Havildar, and some others (Brahmins) lost their lives in the vain attempt to maintain order," (vide *Mofussilite*, August 11.). "It is but too true," says the *Quarterly Review*, April, 1858, "that several faithful Sepoys were bayoneted at their guns in the Bailey Guard Battery (Havelock's first relief of Lucknow) by the infuriated soldiers of the 78th Highlanders who confounded them with other Natives: none of them offered any resistance, and one (afterwards known to have been a Brahmin) whose name should never be forgotten, waved his hand, and with the words—'It is all for the good cause; welcome friend! expired!'"—And where they were not amongst the rebels, they gladly received under their protection any number of European fugitives that fell into their hands, and their conduct as peaceful villagers is throughout marked by that spirit of hospitality and kindness which it is their religious obligation to exhibit to every human being.

CHAPTER V.

An officer of the 38th Native Infantry gives this elaborate account of Brahmin fidelity and assistance by which he, with several friends, passed unscathed through some of the severest struggles on record :—

"Some Brahmins discovered us as they came to work, one took us to the village and put us in a tope (clump of trees) while he got us *chuppaties* (bread) and milk. On the way Mr. Marshall, the auctioneer and merchant, met us. He had quitted the quarter-guard immediately after the Colonel and me, together with three others, but in the morning Marshall alone remained, and where the others are, alive or dead we know not. After giving us food our Brahmin friends took us over a ford of a branch of the Jumna, and concealed us in the long jungle grass on the other side. While there another came to me and said a party of fugitives like ourselves were in the grass at a little distance. I followed, and he led me some two miles, when I found a party of ladies and others concealed. The first person I saw was Proctor, and in my joy at seeing him, whom I had believed shot at the main guard, I saw no one else. After the first joy of meeting him, I looked about and found Mrs. Forest, her husband and three girls, Mrs. Fraser (Engineers), Mr. Salkeld, Vibart and Wilson (Artillery.) I sent to the Colonel and Marshall, and this made our party 13 : with guns and swords we thought ourselves a match for a chance straggling party of mutineers. The escape of this party from the main guard was wonderful. During the afternoon it was determined by Major Abbott at the Cashmere-gate to send what ladies were there to cantonments. There were no conveyances, and they were mounted on the carriages of the guns—who knows what spirit possessed our men ? —they were suddenly dislodged, and a murderous fire commenced on all there assembled. There was a rush up the ramparts into the main guard. Osborne was shot through the thigh ; he said I am not going to be murdered by these Sepoys and led the way throwing himself over the wall into the ditch below, others followed. Mrs. Forest was shot through the shoulder, but over they went, one after another, dropping down what in ordinary circumstances one would say endangered life and limb, yet they reached the ditch, scambled up the scarp, and the party I mention reached Sir T. Metcalf's house the servants gave them some beer and food, and led them to the river bank shortly before the house was fired. They passed such a night as we did with one narrower escape. As they lay concealed some men passed and saw a riband or a bottle, and saying 'Oh, they have been here, evidently, went on.' They came to the same ford, and while concealed heard me descried by my eye-glass, sent for me, and thus we happily met. We could not stay in the grass, so that evening we started, the Brahmins conducting us to a ford over the Jumna. We travelled some two or three miles up stream before reaching it. Our hearts failed, and no wonder, where ladies were concerned, as we looked at the broad swift river. It was getting dark, too. Two natives went across. We watched them anxiously wade a considerable portion of tbe river ; then their heads alone appeared above water. It was our only chance of life, and our brave ladies never flinched. It was so deep that where a tall man would wade, a short man would be drowned. I thought it was all over when, on reaching the deep water with Mrs. Forest on my left arm, a native supporting her on the other side, we were shot down the river ; however, by desperate efforts and assistance by another native, we reached the bank in safety. I swam back once more for another of our party, and so ultimately we all got safe over. It was a brave feat for our ladies to do. We passed another wretched night, suffering fearfully from cold, and crouching close to each other for warmth; there was no noise but the chattering of our teeth. Next morning we were discovered and led to a tope, where again the Brahmins temporarily proved our friends, but they turned us out shortly afterwards with news that there were sowers behind and sowers in front."—*Times, July*, 1857.

It appears that dangers pressed the party too closely to leave them time to breathe. But the Brahmins in this, as in the foregoing instances, were their saviours.

"We were taken to a large Brahmin village that night and concealed in a *fakeer's* hut. We were there three days, and I trust hereafter handsomely to reward our benefactors. While here we sent in a letter in French to Meerut asking for assistance. It seemed not to come, and from Bhekia we were taken to Hurachundpore at the request of an old Zemindar, who had heard of our whereabouts, and treated us royally."—*Ibid.*

Lieut. L. Tucker, late of the 15th Irregular Cavalry, after giving the details of his son's escape from Sultanpore, thus notices the services of the people of a neighbouring village, whose timely assistance and devotedness saved "Charlie" from imminent death :—

"Only fancy how dreadful it was for him to be wandering about in the heat of the day, not knowing where to go and getting people to give him water to drink at wells, and at last drinking it out of little streams he was so terribly thirsty. At last about four o'clock in the afternoon, he asked a man whom he saw for some water and also if he could protect him, for he and his horse were both getting knocked up. The man said he would, and took him into his village and afterwards to his master, who lived in a native fort, and who was the principal person in the place; and there Charlie stayed until the party from here went to fetch him. His escape was most providential, for he did not know the people about there. Soon after he had reached the native's house four others from Sultanpore arrived but one of them knew the way to the person who took Charlie in. He must be a most noble-hearted native, for what we took it half ruined him. He is to have quantities of presents from Charlie, St. George, Henry, and I believe from Government."—*Times*, 17*th Aug.* 1857.

CHAPTER VI.

THE attentive reader will be struck with the thrilling interest of the stories of almost miraculous escapes which the fugitives from

Delhi and other places effected in the face of but too certain death. But he will not fail to mark the undercurrent of a generous feeling, not noisy but gentle, not ostentatious but sincere, springing from a noble desire of rendering service when most needed, to the countrymen of their Most Gracious Sovereign, and also from an abstract love of doing good for good's sake, appearing in all offers of protection and aid made by the peaceably disposed and humane villagers, counterminous to the scenes of rebellion. The following lines taken from a narrative of the escape of Mr. S. H. Batson, Surgeon of the late 74th Native Infantry, instinct with so many incidents of romance that an English writer has been led to pronounce it not unworthy of Defoe, pointedly mark the affectionate simplicity and earnestness with which the villagers received fugitives under their protection :—

" I continued to run along the road towards Kurnaul. I was again stopped by some ironsmiths who were employed in the Delhi Magazine, when one of them said, "Sahib, don't fear, come with me to my village, and I will find you food, if you go on, you will surely be murdered by the Mahomedans who have turned out from the villages to rob and kill the Feringhees." I went with the ironsmiths to their house, and was most humanely and kindly treated, one giving me a *dhottee*, another a cap, another some milk and native bread. I felt my life was safe, I was much excited and could scarcely speak, they gave me a cot, on which I lay down, but could not sleep. I told these people I was a Doctor and in consequence met with much greater attention. On the following morning the *Chowdrie* of the place sent for me, when the whole village assembled to see the "Feringhee doctor". Exhausted as I was, I had to answer a multitude of questions put by the people, but finding I was perfectly acquainted with their religion, languages, and manners, they began to take infinite interest in my life and said they would protect me. While I was staying at this village, I heard Dr. Wood of the 38th Native Infantry, was in a village some 5 or 6 miles off, at one Summeypore; a man from this village came to me and said, "Dr. Wood Sahib is in my village. He requires medicines, as you know all the native medicines, pray, tell me what should be given." I prescribed, but I know not whether the medicines reached him. I also heard while at this village that Colonel Riply was lying wounded at the ice-pit, near the parade ground. I persuaded the villagers that he was a great personage, and that if they would take him food and water; they would be handsomely requited by the Government for their humanity, they took him food several days. A few days afterwards I was in the village of Badree. It was rumored that all the Feringhees of Meerut, Umballah and Calcutta, had been murdered, and that the King of Delhi had taken the Government, and that if any village concealed a Feringhee, it would be death to the owner and general ruin. The proprietors of Badree village got alarmed at this proclamation, and I was removed at night from the village to a small mangoe tope, where I was left night and day. I was visited at night by some one or other of the villagers, who brought me bread and water in a ghurrah. I am unable to describe my feelings during this trying time, I was all day in the sun, in the extreme heat, and alone at night, when the jackals, &c., came prowling about and crying. It is only God and myself know, what I have endured after five days and nights in this tope of trees. I was again taken back to the village and concealed in a Bhoosa-house. I was shut in here for twenty-four hours; the heat and suffocation, I can not find language to describe. I did not know which was the greatest misery, the tope of trees in solitude, or the Bhoosa-kotree. A rumour now was set on foot that several sowars had been deputed to hunt for the Feringhees in the different villages and it was considered prudent that I quit Badree under the escort of a *Fuqeer-Joghee.* This man came and offered to convey me anywhere, that I might please, but stated that it was not a safe moment for me to remain where I was. I then started for Bursooah, where I remained the night. this Fuqueer and his friends dyed all my clothes, and gave me necklaces of beads (Roodrach) &c., to assume the garb of a Fuqueer myself. After making all preparations to pass as a Fukeer, I commenced my pilgrimage with him. He took me to several villages and passed me off as a Cashmere, "Dadoo Puntoe Fuqueer Joghee." In all the villages that I passed, I was cross-questioned, but understanding their Jotish religion and oaths, I met with every kindness, some giving me pice, others food. The Hindoos all expressed the most merciful feelings towards the Feringhees, while the Mahomedans could not disguise their murderous feelings. I was taken to a village to the house of a Sewak Doss, Sunt Fuqueer Kuberee, understanding his code of religion and being able to recite several Kubberee kubbits, he received me in every kindness. I told him I was a Cashmeree, but the sage could not reconcile his mind that I was a Cashmeree with the blue eyes. He said your language, gesture, clothes, &c., are all complete, but your blue eyes betray you, you are surely a Feringhee. I disclosed to him what I was, nevertheless, as I had acquired the kubera oaths, he continued to believe the same. While I was sitting at this Fuqueer's place, a sepoy came saying, he

had letters he was taking to the Umballah force that was at Rau. He did not discover that I was a Feringhee, but I disclosed him that I was a Doctor Sahib, would he take my letter to the officer commanding the force. I gave him a letter soliciting assistance, which he most faithfully conveyed, but after waiting a day in hopes of getting assistance, and none coming, I thought it prudent to proceed twoards Meerut; the beggar who had conducted me thus far, volunteered to take me on. Several people of this village accompanied me till we got to Hurchundpore, where a Mr. Francis Cohen, a Zemindar (originally a tussildar, in the Government employment,) resides. This old gentleman received me in all kindness, and showed me the certificates under the signature of Colonel Knyvett, Captain Salkeld, Lieutenant Holland, Mr. Marshal, Merchant of Delhi, and others setting forth that they had received every kindness from Mr. Cohen, who had kindly sent them on to Meerut. I then made arrangements to proceed to Meerut when a letter was brought from Kaykrah village to my address, telling me that a hundred men of the Jheend Rajah's force, commanded by Captain MacAndrews, was waiting at Kaykrah to take me on to Rau, where the Head Quarters were."
—*Times*, *17th August*, *1857*.

CHAPTER VII.

A Lady writing from Agra, says that when the rising at Gwalior took place, the fidelity of their servants only served her husband, herself and family from falling into the hands of the rebels. If the mutiny has applied a too severe test to the loyalty of the people, it has also subjected to no less hard a trial the fidelity of domestic servants. And it is gratifying to observe that the issue has been honorable to both parties. Had it not been for their unswerving attachment, we may confidently say, half the European residents would, ere long, have been numbered with the dead. The aid which they offered, if not effectual for the purpose or adequate to the need, was yet too important to be forgotten by those who received it. While the country was strewed with corpses and raging with fire—while despair sat upon every brow and treachery the dread of the hour—one kind word—one hint to help—was a world of aid and benefit, and the value of it could be appreciated only by those who felt the anger of the season. Apropos to this we may mention on the authority of the *Times* that when two companies of Col. Troup's regiment surrounded his house to shoot him, he was warned by his bearer, fled through a back door, jumped on his horse and galloped off!

An Officer writing from Azimgurh thus describes how he and his party were treated by the people of Goruckpore :—

"We were in Goruckpore on Sunday the 19th, and took up thence the ladies of the station, consisting of the wives of three Civilians and of a Captain commanding there. There fortunately, were only a few more than hundred in number, but they formed part of the 17th Regiment who had been stationed here at Azimghur, and had plundered the treasury and left the district. There was a distrust of these Sepoys, who, had they not been overawed by some Irregular Cavalry and some armed men belonging to a Rajah, would have mutinied also. At Goruckpore, through the kindness of the people we were supplied with wearing apparel, sufficient to carry on for a few days. We left, as I said, on the evening of Sunday, with an immense cavalcade, composed of baggage, carriers, carriages, sowars or Irregular Cavalry and a party of armed natives belonging to the Rajah. We travelled by torch light in dreadful confusion, as we are escaping for our lives through districts where the population was hostile, and where Europeans had been previously murdered. As yet however, we have got on extremely well, the escort of Irregular Cavalry, whom we feared more than an enemy from without, have hitherto behaved well and promise to do so."—*Times, 24th August*, 1857.

The gallant brother of Gordon Cumming, the Lion-hunter, gives the following lively account of his men's fidelity.

"The men say themselves, they would not trust their own fathers now-a-days. I get on with them very well, though my *jemadar* is a capital fellow, and Bappas is invaluable. Neither of them ever seems tc tire, they are constantly moving about among the men, armed with double rifles, swords and pistols. When I was in the jungle, one or two of my party showed signs of warning, but the rest swore they would shoot down any man who attempted that kind of humbug. I have raised the pay of all the police and sowars and have sent fifteen men to Mhow to-day to get some muskets and ammunition which have been promised to me by Elliott."—*Times, 31st August*, 1857.

CHAPTER VIII.

This interesting little story of the offer of assistance by a party of Bheels, is mixed up with a strangeness and simplicity of manner, characterstic of the doings of savages on occasions when their hospitable feelings are called into play :—

"A Bheel, who had observed what was going on, carried intelligence to the nearest town, a small place called Para, of the invasion by the Umghura people. Firing at the insult, a party started from Para to drive them away. Just as the gray of the morning appeared, we had the pleasure of being rescued by them, and thus did God raise up instruments for our delivery when death seemed near at hand. But had the villians not been such cowards, nothing could have saved us, if they had attacked us in the night. This fresh party carried us to Para, and were civil enough at first, and towards evening, for some reason or other, they began to get very insolent and commenced plundering us. We saw our position had but little improved and we prepared again to sell our lives as dearly as could be. But just as things appeared to be getting desperate, a party arrived from Jabua, 10 miles away, sent by the Chief to our rescue, as soon as he had heard of our being at Para. They carried us to Jabua that same evening, and we reached the town early in the morning, having rested for some hours on the road. The young Chief, who is a very pleasing looking boy, of 16 or 17, received us very kindly. The managing authority, however, is an old lady, who is, I believe, grandmother to the Chief, and by her directions everything that could be done for our safety or comfort was effected."—*Times*, 31*st August*, 1857.

Mr. J. P. Gubbins of Benares, thus brings forward prominently, through the medium of the *Times*, the conspicuous acts of loyalty of Rajah Soorut Singh :—

" Rajah Soorut Singh, a Sikh Chieftain, who was living at Benares under a slight surveillance at the time of the mutinies, and who was on intimate terms with my brother, used his exertions successfully to keep a company of his countrymen steady, who were on guard at the Mint, where all the ladies and children were collected and has since proved himself so brave and true that the Europeans have subscribed £100, in order to present him with a handsome set of fire arms."—*Times*, 31*st August*, 1857.

Here is an instance of protection proffered by the peasants of Guraon, the interest of which is scarcely surpassed by the records of chivalrous gallantry of the Middle Ages, or the adventures in Italian and Spanish romances. Services rendered under ordinary circumstances, though valuable, cannot approach in importance to those which are offered under difficulties like the one under notice. Here was a young woman whose person was coveted by the Chief of the place. There was not a single European to look after her, but the good peasants, inspired as it were by Providence, espoused her innocent cause and at the risk of their lives and property, manfully stood in her behalf. If Mrs. Nun is still in the land of the living, which we earnestly hope to be the case, she should, as becomes her gratitude and moral sense, come forward and name the persons who so heroically saved her life and honor. The call is imperative and we trust it will be satisfied. The story is given by the officer to whose camp she was carried after three months of concealment and friendly protection.

"I was on the picket on the 31st of July, and had come back from my first patrol when, on reaching one of my videttes, he told me that he had just passed a European woman with two children escorted by some natives into my picket. I cantered on and overtook a country cart escorted by by some villagers, one of whom carried a poor little boy about four years old on his shoulder. In the cart I found a nice voung looking woman with a little infant. The poor creature seemed overjoyed to see a European face, and, in answer to my queries, told me that she was the wife of a Mr. Nun, son of the riding master of the first Cavalry. Her husband was employed in the Customs Department, at a place near Guzgaon. When the outbreak at Delhi took place he was in the district with Ford, of the Civil Service. By untoward circumstances in this troubled time, this unhappy woman was left by herself, without a European near her. The instant the people of the village nearest her house heard that parties of Sepoys were coming in their direction, they carried off Mrs. Nun, with her children, and concealed them in their village. Parties of horsemen arrived and enquired for her, and on being told that she had gone off, plundered and burnt her house. To make a long story short, these poor fellows at the risk of their lives, kept this unhappy family for three months, feeding and clothing them, and hurrying them off to other villages, whenever they heard of the approach of any parties of the mutineers. I must tell you that the insurgents offered 100 rnpees reward for Mrs. Nun, dead or alive, but nothing would tempt these simple ryots to betray their trust; and, finally, having seized an opportunity, they brought them safely into camp. The poor woman spoke most gratefully of their kindness and devotion, and the little boy seemed to have the greatest affection for the grey-headed old man, on whose shoulder he was perched."—*Times, 2nd Oct.* 1857.

The friends of Mr. William Edwards of the Bengal Civil Service, whose name was returned in the list of casualties, in contradicting the statement, thus notice his escape:—

"The list of casualties in your paper of this evening, copied from the Homeward Mail, contains the name William Edwards, Bengal Civil Service. The family of that gentleman have received letters by this mail of the 9th and 11th of August, informing them of his safety, along with Mr. Probyn, of the Civil Service, and his family under the protection of a friendly zemindar, by whom they were kindly treated, when the strictest concealment was requisite."—*Times,, 2nd October*, 1857.

A Bengal Civilian, in reporting to the *Times*, the condition of the Behar Division of the Bengal Presidency, has the following about Chupra and Cheybassa:—

"There has been no outrage and no plunder there, because of the spirit and loyalty of a Mahomedan resident, well known in those parts, and (hitherto) always doubted—a certain Cazy Ramzan Allee. He assumed the command on the departure of the Europeans, kept every thing quiet and loyal, and has since delivered over his charge, prisoners and all, in perfect order to the returned Civilians. He and others similarly behaved well, you may be sure, be handsomely rewarded."—*Times.*

CHAPTER IX.

THE details of the services of this loyal Mahomedan are given in the correspondence which passed between him and the Government of Bengal, extracts from which will be found further on. This man, in the midst of his unswerving fidelity was calumniated anonymously in the public papers, but his sense of duty was so strong that he, regardless of the calumnies, went on in his useful career which has justly entitled him to the gratitude of the Government.

Among the many valuable communications on the Indian Mutinies which the *Times* has published, there are few which display such an acuteness and accuracy of observation, such marvellous correctness of fact, such faithful details of the history of the revolt, and so dispassionate and thoughtful an analysis of the causes of the rebellion—as the letter written by a military Officer from Umballa. In treating its readers with this masterly production, the *Times* prefaces that it is written by a "gentleman whose acquirements, experience and position admirably qualify him for the work of observation and review. Our readers, we are sure, (continues the leading journal,) will be deeply interested in the perusal of so lucid and comprehensive a memoir." Indeed an Indian Journalist, occupying no mean position in the roll of journalistic fame, once suggested that if the Government contemplated to give the world a history of the revolt, it should forthwith entertain the services of the gentleman whose eminent abilities displayed in that letter deservedly point him out for the work. We therefore need make no apology for the following from which the reader will perceive the exact nature of the rebellion and the position of the people in reference thereto :—

"In the evening of the day of the Delhi outbreak, the survivors in cantonments finding themselves gradually deserted by their men and without aid from Meerut, determined to fly. They had a number of carriages of different kinds, most of them took the road to Kurnaul, some few that to Meerut, and they generally escaped in safety. Other stragglers from various quarters had more difficult and perilous escapes, wandering fugitives from village, some were thus wandering for several weeks before they reached European relatives, and they endured most cruel hardships of want and weather. But generally the behaviour of the villagers was kind ; many sheltered and assisted—none actually attacked them. This Brahmin villagers in particular—there are a good many agricultural Brahmin villages scattered about that part of the country, showed them the greatest kindness, and gave them active protection."—*Times*, *26th October*, 1857.

The following is an extract from a letter from George Palmer Esq., of the Bengal Civil Service :—

"I am living now in the house of the chief merchant of this town. It is lonely enough to have

English face to look at, or talk to, especially in these times, but still I am very thankful that I am as well in health as I am, notwithstanding hard work, exposure and sun. I am very fortunate, too, in having my old Punjaubi servant and his brother with me. Though at a distance from their own houses, and though Mossulmans, and though subjected to every kind of temptation, they have served me most faithfully, and I trust them as my own kith and kin. If any thing should happen to me in these days, pray do not forget to do something for them. The eldest is my Zamandar. His name is Syad Ameer, son of Sheik Rookeen-od-deene, of Kalmore, in the district of Gordaspore."—*Times, 9th November*, 1857.

Here is an interesting account of the good feeling and readiness of villagers to assist European fugitives :—

"We are still in a state of uncertainty and anxiety, but our hopes have lately been much removed by the discovery of one of the officers of his regiment (the 18th) Lieutenant Gowan, the Adjutant, who was one of the missing, a servant of his having found him concealed in some village. He sent a letter by him to Colonel——, at Nynee Tal, giving an account of his escape, and how he got separated from the rest of the party after the few well-disposed Sepoys had saved them on the day of the outbreak. He had gone through a great deal, but expresses himself very thankful for the protection and kindness he had received from some Hindus, by whom he was still secreted. He had heard that several Europeans were in concealment in different villages, which native spies and others who are friendly to the English also confirm and say that a Banker at Bareily has secretly supplied them with money"—*Ibid.*

This party of nearly thirty persons, consisting of men, women and children, were protected, fed, and sheltered by a Rajah at Gopalpore. The character of the service may well be imagined when we mention that he not only gave this protection, but with his men escorted the party to a place of security amidst brother Europeans :—

" We are now with a friendly Rajah at Gopalpore on the river, twenty-five miles from Goruckpore ; he has promised to send us to Dinapore, which is distant 120 miles. I believe we are now quite safe, though we have been in danger, and suffered much discomfort and misery. Our party consists of Captain and Mrs. Reid, and 2 children ; Captain and Messrs. Orr and sister, and 5 children; and Messrs. Thurburn and 1 child ; Captain and Mrs. Dawson and 4 children ; Mr. and Mrs. Bradford

Mr. and Mrs. Fitzgerald and child, and Mr. and Mrs. Hurst and child."—*Ibid.*

A letter from Captain Orr, dated Gopalpore, near Gograh, June 24th, mentions

"That he and his family, with Miss Troup and the rest of his party who escaped from Fyzabad, had reached Gopalpore in safety, and expected to be at Dinapore on the 29th. They were to proceed under the protection of the Rajah of Gopalpore, who has shown himself faithful to the British Government.

* * * * *

Mrs. Black, Mrs. Goldney, and Mrs. Strahan were brought into Allahabad, by that noble fellow Ajeet Singh, who saw Lieutenant Grant and the party of 37 Europeans, who accompanied him from his camp near Fyzabad."—*Ibid.*

CHAPTER X.

A WRITER describing the mutiny of the 17th Native Infantry at Azimghur, thus gives the story of the escape of the party of Europeans who were then at that station :—

"We were at breakfast, when we were surrounded by about 400 men, armed and unarmed, and with great difficulty we escaped with our lives, and for 14 long and weary days, were living in a cowshed, protected by the Zemindars of a large Hindu village; the people behaved to us with the utmost kindness, and gave us flour, *dal*, meat, &c. to exist upon."—*Englishman*, *2nd July*, 1857.

A Correspondent says :—

"I don't know-whether it will be news to you, that the undermentioned officers, ladies, &c., arrived at Dinapore on the 29th June, from Fyzabad.

Captain Dawson and wife,
" Reid and wife,
" Orr and wife,
" Thurburn and wife,

with (15) fifteen children, some Serjeants and their wives, they were nearly naked, starving and suffering from Opthalmia. They had been for some days under the protection of Rajah Maun Singh, who had treated them well."—*Englishman*, *6th July*, 1857.

Of the services of Maun Singh, which were neither few nor small, we have spoken in detail in another place We would here simply remark that these did not extend to the protection and sheltering of European fugitives only, an assumption of which has led some opponents of the Rajah to construe his position into a doubtful neutrality ; his conduct is throughout marked by a complete isolation from the rebels and this, above all, shows that he cherished no sympathies for the cause of the insurgents.

The following is from a Correspondent in the Sagour and Nerbuddah Territories, dated the 25th June :—

"I have just heard from a person who has arrived from Benares, that whilst en route from Rewah to Myheeree, he saw a party of some twenty-five ladies and gentlemen, in a variety of costumes, from the elegant and simple night dress, to the ordinary shooting jacket. On enquiry, I learnt that the flying Brigade was from the direction of Nowgong and Banda. They had evidently to cut and run for it, judging from their appearance ; I understand that had it not been for the kind assistance of the Rewah Rajah, they would have been in a fix. The Rajah, I believe, has placed a large party of horse under Lieutenant Osborne, a cousin, I am informed, of Lieutenant Willoughby, the officer who so gallantly blew up the Delhi Arsenal."—*Englishman, 6th July*, 1857.

The writer of the following was one of

the fugitives from Fyzabad. From his statement it appears that he and his party were entirely indebted for their lives to the kind exertions of Rajah Kessenkissore Chand of Gopalpore and his people :—

"After this we went on land, and having met a fisherman, we found out that there was a well disposed native (Rajah Kessenkissore Chand of Gopalpore) not far off; that he had there some Europeans under his protection. We made for this man's place, and next day he gave us 25 men, and we and the other Europeans started for Dinapore. These Europeans had been attacked two days before by another Rajah, but were defended by Kessenkissore, and they told us that if we had landed two days before, we should certainly have been murdered by the other Rajah's people."—*Englishman, 6th July*, 1857.

A letter from Gorruckpore, 20th ultimo, says :—

"Colonel Lennox and family are safe ; they have just left this, and many officers and ladies, with some of the non-Commissioned Officers, have proceeded in safety towards Dinapore, escorted by Maun Singh's own men. The country seems to be quiet. The Rajahs, almost all, are flocking in, with large bodies of men, to support Government, and we are daily expecting Nepaul troops to pass through ; a few may remain to restore order."—*Englishman, 7th July*, 1857.

The following is from Ghazeepore, dated 7th July :—

"Colonel and Mrs. Lennox have been here some days, I believe they are from Fyzabad. Mr. and Mrs. Bradford from the same station came in yesterday, having gone through many hardships, and had narrow escapes, he is indebted to his tussildar for having saved him and Mrs, B."—*Englishman, 7th July*, 1857.

Again,

"Report says the Rajah of Lalpoorah has sent five hundred men to protect the station, 50 men from the 65th left this some days ago for Azimghur."—*Englishman, 7th July*, 1857.

CHAPTER .XI.

THE Bengal army is gone, but its memory is associated with not a few names of proved loyalty and attachment which stand in bold and agreeable relief to the heartless conduct of the misguided majority. Instances not few in number are recorded of Sepoys who, deaf to the persuasions and entreaties of their brethren and true to the calls of duty and gratitude, became the most active agents in the salvation of many officers. These heroes distinguished alike by moral courage and physical bravery will each and all, we trust, receive the full meed of approbation from the future chronicler of the revolt and from the distant posterity. And a grateful Government which has already rewarded the services of some of the faithful, will not forget the numerous others who, though they have not so prominently distinguished themselves, are yet entitled to every consideration which an unflinching conduct, through so dreadful an ordeal as the Indian insurrection presented, richly deserves. Mr. Russel, the *Times*' Correspondent, in one of his celebrated letters from the Seat of War, very properly remarks that the British Government has been "waging war against Hindoos and Mussalmans by the aid and with the consent of Hindoos and Mussalmans, just as Alexander was

5

able to beat Porus by the aid of his Indian allies, and no European or other State can rule in India without the co-operation and assistance of a large proportion, of the races which inhabit the vast peninsula." Though the aid and fidelity of wealthy and influential zeminders, allied Princes and of the people in and near the disturbed districts, and the quiet demeanour of the mass of the population, anxiously awaiting for the end of the struggle, which vexatiously interfered with the smooth career of their peaceful lives, have materially helped our rulers in overcoming this crisis, still the unswerving fidelity of particular men of every regiment was of no ordinary service. Coupled with the fact that though by blood and position these faithful men are kinsmen and companions of those who raised the standard of revolt, yet they have remained true to their salt, their allegiance has been made doubly sure by acts which no hypocrisy would condescend to, and which no motives short of sense of duty and gratitude could lead to. They have been also especially valuable as they have served reliable guides in many instances from the circumstance of their having attended the councils of mutiny, and having conversed with the feelings and motives of their unfortunate brethren, without of course participating in their plots. The following is a prominent instance of services of the kind under comment :—

"That there are some good and loyal men in every Regiment, I will admit, and the following little incident that has just occurred, will prove, I think, that the 73rd has one man at least true to his salt. Lieutenant Dandridge, who is the adjutant of the Regiment, sent up one of the Sepoys, an old Brahmin, in charge of his wife and property. This man was invited by some of the Hindu Native officers, attached to our Sebundees, to dine with them ; which invitation was accepted, and the Brahmin of the 73rd, dined with them. In the course of the after-dinner conversation, some seditious talk was entered upon as I have heard to the following effect :—That these native officers wished some others would join them in exterminating the Europeans, that they were but few themselves, and that the men of their corps would never join them, would rather assist the Europeans than otherwise. After this dinner was over, the Brahmin of the 73rd went straight off to the adjutant of the Depot and reported the matter fully, and, yesterday these fellows were seized, a Court of Enquiry was immediately held, the result of which I have not yet learned, further than they are all there kept close prisoners in three different places, two of them under an European guard, and the third in the guard of his own lines. The old Brahmin should be rewarded."—*Englishman, 7th July.*

Numerous instances have transpired of such good men and true assisting their European Officers under difficulties before which ordinary humanity would most probably sink. Some of these the reader will meet with as he will proceed. *En passant* we may mention here that when the mutiny at Fyzabad occurred, Captain Lennox and others were enabled through the fidelity of two friendly Sepoys, to effect their escape to the seat of a kind chieftain after a series of adventures the most serious and thrilling.

A letter from Mozufferpore, Tirhoot, dated 4th July, says :—

"The only officers who have bestirred themselves to any purpose, are the Magistrate and his assistant, the latter gentleman being particularly energetic and public spirited. Nor I must omit to mention the praiseworthy conduct of our second

Principal Sudder Ameen who, at a great expense, entertained as guests, for several days, a large number of Planters assembled here for the protection of the Station, while those who had invited them for that purpose, held themselves aloof, and exhibited their usual amount of illiberal pride, obtuseness of judgment and narrow-minded parsimony.' *Englishman*, 10*th July*, 1857.

We extract with pleasure the following two paragraphs from the *Englishman* : they betoken a zeal for service to the British Government only surpassed by the effects achieved :—

" The Rajah of Keroula has issued a proclamation, warning his subjects, under penalty of death, not to join or assist the rebels, but to fight with fidelity under European Officers, whenever they may be called upon to do so."—*Englishman*, 15*th July*, 1857.

The reader will not overlook the importance of the service noted below, because the intelligence is conveyed in two brief lines :—

" The Maharaja of Rewah* has supplied

---

* The position of the Rajah was peculiarly critical from almost the commencement of the mutiny, but with a courage,

Lieutenant W. Osborne with a detachment for the protection of Mirzapore."—*Ibid.*

The following is from Secunderabad, dated 5th July :—

"Shumshaool Oomrah is, I believe, his (the Nizám's) chief adviser, and a right good one ; he is well affected towards us, he will take good care in company with Salar Jung that the Nizam is not tainted with any evil counsels. The minister most certainly deserves some substantial mark of regard from the British Government, for to him only we are indebted for the hitherto quiet keeping of the city. Wherever disorder has been inclined to raise its head, the Arabs have been slipped, and the instigators apprehended and punished. It is premature in these days of doubt and uncertainty to commit oneself to say too much, but unless any thing very unlooked for occurs, I think we may felicitate ourselves in having passed the crisis."—*Englishman*, 17*th July*, 1857.

We entirely concur with the writer of the above in the praise he accords to the English-educated Minister of the Nizam.

---

resolution, and judgment not common among Oriental princes, nursed on the lap of luxury, he passed through the crisis with honor to himself and advantage to the British Government.—*Compiler.*

We have dwelt at length in another place on the distinguished talents, unflinching courage and sterling statesmanship which he has displayed throughout the crisis in Hydrabad.

A letter from Meerut, dated the 20th June, says :

"All the Sirsa Europeans, with the poor Captain Hillard, and another officer who placed blind confidence in the savage natives, were obliged to flee from that place on the 30th of last month, and reached Putteeallah on the 12th instant. They were kindly treated by the Maharajah, who immediately on their arrival, procured clean clothes for them all, they having had the one suit of clothes on from the day of their escape to that on which they arrived at Putteeallah.

Were in not for the noble way in which the Maharajah acted, they would never have been able to have made their escape from the Sirsa district. From Putteealla two of the party made a run into Umballah, to consult the Commissioner of that place on certain matters, and returned to Putteeallah again, from which place they were preparing to start, accompanied by their companions in danger, and the Maharajah's Forces for Sirsa."—*Mofussilite*, quoted by the *Englishman*.

To this excellent ally of the British

Government the success before Delhi throughout the memorable siege, which the *Times* characterizes as having broken the neck of the revolt, is in no small measure indebted. We have reviewed his services more fully in a separate place.

The following is a curious piece of romance not rare in the events of this memorable insurrection :—

"The Julda Rajah, who was imprisoned at Hazareebaugh for 14 years, was liberated by the Sepoys; he made his way home, collected some 800 men and stopped the Sepoys, who were making off with the Poorooliah treasure 108,000 Rupees. It is not known if the Sepoys made a fight for it, but it is asserted the Rajah holds the money for the Government."—*Englishman, 11th August*, 1857.

The following is from Govindpore, dated the 23rd August :—

"On the 20th instant a detachment of Seikhs, with an officer, halted at the Govindpore encamping ground. They are, I am told by the officer in command, going to Gyah, and will remain there until further orders. The Zemindar of Punchkote is, in this critical period; helping the Government, and has sent about 70 Sowars and some Sepoys to put down the disturbances at

Manbhoom, where depredation is the order of the day.

* * * * * * * * *

The Rajah of Serakelah has saved the treasure of Singhbhoom by his own men and has applied to the Bengal Government for 2,000 Rupees to raise and equip a Regiment to preserve peace on the South-west Frontier.—*Englishman*, *26th August*, 1857.

A correspondent in the vicinity of Patna, says among other things :—

"That Shah Kobuooddeen has proposed to place a body of cavalry at the service of Government."—*Englishman*, *29th August*, 1857.

The following is anent the aid which the troops present at the Bareilly skirmish received from the neighbouring villagers :—

" We then went on till about 10 P. M., when halt was called, some charpoys were got from a neighbouring village, as well as some food and water for the horses, we loosened their girths, which must have been a great relief to them, and having got men to hold our horses, we laid down to rest, with the intention of taking a nap for two or three hours but we had not been there an hour when it was determined to go on, so we mounted again."—*Ibid.*

CHAPTER XII.

If military revolutions are ever famed for levelling all distinctions of rank and fortune and forestalling all the sufferings of indigence and helplessness, the Sepoy outbreak has formed no exception to the universal rule. If it has occasioned a loss of life and blood unequalled in the annals of British India, it has entailed a loss of property equally unprecedented. In an uncontrolled play of the impulses of a Pretorian body like the Bengal Army, the marauding and predatory habits of the Goojur and other tribes of professional plunderers were naturally called into action, and the results, as was expected, have been quite distracting. It was then that the collected scoundrelism of the jails, the feelings of which had been long pent up under an effective Prison discipline, found a licensed vent to spread destruction over the country. It converted the crusade of the Sepoys against Europeans and Christians into a crusade against the wealth and property of the landholders. Thus every man, whether European or Native, under any circumstances calculated to awaken suspicion, was a prey to its rapacity. Hence during the most gloomy period of the crisis streams of fugitives, shorn of the last farthing and destitute of every earthly possession poured forth into this city, to awaken the sympathy of the people. Fellow-feeling and benevolence, without any loss of time, led the citizens to band together and to raise voluntary contributions among themselves for the support and relief of the sufferers. And the Natives with their wonted liberality joined the movement. Persons in all ranks and stations of life have equally, each according to his own means contributed in aid of the Relief Fund. An organized Committee has been formed to employ the fund to its legitimate purposes, and it numbers four Native gentlemen among its members. In distributing the aid of the fund the European portion of the Committee has limited it to Christian sufferers only, but the Native Members have, notwithstanding this invidious and unjust distinction, lent their active and cordial co-operation to the working out of this benevolent scheme. Princely contributions have been received from many Indian Princes and Chieftains, and altogether the amount of indigenous Indian aid forms a quite respectable sum and not unworthy of the fame of Hindoostan. In some instances too the princely donations of Indian Potentates have been respectfully refused, and a moderate sum at the suggestion of British Residents has been accepted. The following is a case in point :—

"We learn from the Madras papers, that the Rajah of Travancore has offered the sum of thirty thousand rupees to the fund for the relief of the sufferers by the Mutinies. The Resident accepted only 5,000 five thousand."—*Englishman*, 5*th Sept.*, 1857.

The services of this Rajah were considerable and they will be found fully described in our extracts from the Parliamentary papers on the Indian Mutinies.

letter from Singhbhoom, dated 2nd instant, mentions that the Rajah of Serakelah kept all quiet and peaceable in that quarter. All workmen had returned to their labor, and it was evident that the natives were now beginning to think that the British would still reign supreme in India as heretofore."—*Englishman*, 11*th Sept.*, 1857.

A party from Cawnpore was thus protected and taken care of by a neighbouring Rajah :—

"When he had gone about 6 miles, firing on both sides ceased, and soon after we were hailed by some natives on the outside, who asked us to come on shore, and said that they would take us to their Rajah who was friendly to the English. We gave ourselves up and were taken six miles in land to the Rajah who treated us very kindly, giving us clothes and food. We stayed with him for about a month as he would not let us leave, saying that the roads are unsafe. At last he sent us off on the 29th July to the right bank of the river to a zemindar of a village who got us a hackery"—*Ibid.*

The following is taken from an account of the mutiny at Kolapore :—

"Government and the European Society of Kolapore have much reason to thank the Sowars of Southern Marhatta Irregular horse for their bravery, gallantry and fidelity. One of the Native Officers of the horse has been promoted to the highest grade of Commissioned Officer, and a trooper to the highest rank of non-commissioned. Captain Kerr has been thanked by the Kolapore authorities, and we trust that Government will not forget the deep debt they owe him. It is satisfactory to know that the Rajah of Kolapore lent Colonel Maugham three guns to try and breach the walls of the enemies' position. They were two hundred years old, and the shot only a third of the calibre, hence useless. 200 rounds were fired, but all to no purpose. The Rajah and all the country are loyal."—*Bombay Telegraph and Courier*, quoted by the *Englishman*.

A letter dated Fort Agra, the 4th of September, says :—

"We have secured the co-operation of a loyal zemindar, who is at the head of a force of well disposed natives, including 2,000 horse, and the writer adds that we may now safely calculate the chances of success of the rebels in this quarter to be very small."—*Englishman, 19th September,* 1858.

The following is a marked instance of the promptness and alacrity with which Natives in all parts of the country have come forward to assist Government with men and money at this unparalleled crisis, both political and financial :

"Small notes from one Rupee to five, have been issued by the Superintendent, we however have been more fortunate; no such expedient was found necessary here, for Lord William Hay has filled the treasury of Simla from the purses of the Ranahs and Rajahs of the Hills, also from those of the Bunneahs and Mohajuns of the Bazar. These have all been called upon to lend their superfluous cash to Government on interest. This demand of course is not compulsory, still those who respond to the call willingly and liberally, will thus prove their friendship to Government and may expect favor in times to come. The Bunneahs of the Nalaghur Bazar, have contributed 8,000 Rupees. The Ranah of Bulson, the senior chieftain (the head of five generations now living) took the lead in forwarding the assistance. The Rajah of Sirmoor and Kilmoor, almost all of the minor chieftains, have likewise added to our public purse, as was the case during the Cabul campaign."—*Englishman, 25th September*, 1857.

CHAPTER XIII.

WE extract the following passages from the painfully interesting narrative of Lieutenant Jackson, 12th Regiment Native Infantry, regarding the escape of a Nowgong party after leaving Churrutpore :

" On leaving Mahobah, as above mentioned, it had been our intention to have halted at a village named Muddunpore (Chutterpore) but owing to the badness of the roads, and our being greatly incommoded with some ten or twelve carts (mostly containing the families of the Drummers, &c., we only found ourselves at sunrise, on the morning of the 18th, at the village of Joorah (Mahola), where we halted for the day. Shortly after our arrival, we were joined by Mr. Corn, Collector at Mahobah, who brought with him one thousand Rupees, which had been lent us by the Rajah of Chircurrah, and with money the native officers and men with us were paid up in full for the month of May, 1857, in the course of the day.

"That night, the 20th, just at sunset, we arrived at a village on the road from Allahabad to Banda, which turned out to be the only one which we had seen, which had not turned out against us directly we were seen. We were treated with great kindness and on the morning of the 21st, again set off, having two guides to show us the way to Kallinuggur, where we had been advised to go to and thence to Nagode.

"A little before sunset we most fortunately arrived amongst some other villagers, eight in number, who had determined to stick by each other, and remain faithful to the Government. Had we not thus providentially fallen amongst friends at this moment, we could not have held out much longer as my horse was scarcely able to get along, as we must have come that day, I should say, forty-five miles, and a great deal of the distance at a hard gallop. We were treated most hospitably; the next day, the 22nd, removed to a stronger and a larger village from whence I despatched a letter to the Ranee of Ajeegurh, requesting protection, which was immediately granted, and we arrived at that place a distance of about 10 or 12 miles on the 23rd, being guarded on our way by matchlock-men provided from the village we had been stopping at. At Ajeegurh, we remained till the morning of the 28th June, as Mr. Kurschoff was unable to stand from fatigue, and both ourselves and horses required rest. On the 28th, we started for Nagode, the Ranee of Ajeegurh having lent us elephants, and arrived there on the 29th June 1857."—*Englishman, 28th September*, 1857.

The following passages are taken from an account of the experiences of the second party that fled from Nowgong, and which separated from the main body on their taking the Banda road, by G. Langdale, late clerk to Captain P. G. Scott, 12th N. I. Station Staff and in charge of Military treasure chest, Nowgong :—

"I had scarcely become resigned to my fate, when a man came to me as a Rajah's messenger, with an invitation to go to him. I was completely unprepared for such good fortune, and availed myself of it most hopefully. The Rajah of Loogasie treated me very kindly, he asked numerous questions about the mutiny at Nowgong, and seemed very solicitous for the safety of the officers. He enquired if any of them had been killed, but I had to state my inability to satisfy any of his enquiries respecting the mutiny, through the circumstances under which I had been obliged to escape. He ordered me some food and directed his servant to have me accommodated for the night in a house in the village, particularly desiring no one to be allowed to molest me. He sent for me next morning to say that he was about to write to Major Kirke at Chutturpore and intended sending a spy to Nowgong, to see if the mutineers had deserted the place.

"On the night of the third day, we left Mohubba to go to Killengur. Our first march was to the village of Jorai. Here we met Mr. Karne, the Assistant Magistrate of Hameerpore, who brought us 1,000 rupees, which had been lent by the Rajah of Chirkanee.

"The report about the villagers of Kubari intending to assault us was evidently intended to drive us away, but I cannot explain by whom it was raised, probably the Sepoys tired of their work, prompted it. At all events I was told they advised the officers to leave.

"Some device must have been at the bottom,

for the report turned out quite false. We remained at that village for twelve or thirteen days, being supplied with food by the natives, but as the supply was very scanty, we used to get diet prepared for ourselves by the Bhuttoriwa, or man in charge of the Serai where we put up.

"After being turned out of Rubrai we bent our course in the direction of Mitown, on the way to Banda, we reached that village at six in the evening and were treated by the villagers with exceeding compassion, they met us on entering the village, led us into it, asking the usual questions and provided food and charpoys (Native beds). We asked the zemindars to allow us to remain four or five days, they hospitably answered, "stay as long as you like". The zemindars extended their kindness even to making us up a suit of clothes each, and presenting blankets to every one of us; the very Bunneas (grain dealers) who are proverbially a hard-hearted race, supplied us with grain and flour by turns, some of the people gave tobacco graciously also, our small party being quite unanimous about the unadvisability of proceeding to Banda, owing to the accounts we heard of the murder of Europeans there, I wrote to Major Ellis, Political Assistant of Bundlecund, soliciting assistance to enable us to reach Nagode. The zemindars gave a messenger one rupee to convey this letter, and he returned in ten days, with a note for me from Captain Scott, and a native letter to the zemindars from Mr. Ellis, promising them a future reward for their care of us. We left Morown after a stay of nearly a month, on the 12th August, with a guard of fifty men for our protection to Nagode. Reaching Gowrecher, a distance of fifteen miles, we were pressed to pass some time there by Rajah Dhur, the Jagirdar of that place. His invitation was so cordial, that we could not doubt his good-will by a refusal, and his subsequent liberality induced us to stay there for seventeen days, during which he sent to Banda for tailors to make us some clothes, and cloth to make them of; he also sent for plates, tumblers, basins, &c., for our use. The man despatched was unsuccessful, through a quarrel that had arisen between the Nawab of Banda and Dawa Saheb, the Kamdar of the Ranee of Ajeeghur, a neighbouring territory.

"The only thing the servant brought from Banda was shoes, which were too large for us and had to be returned. The Rajah munificently instructed his people to provide us with every thing we desired, irrespective of any reference to him. We left him with many expressions of our gratitude on the 28th August, 1857. He provided the females in our company with his palkees, and mounted us on an elephant."—*Englishman, 2nd October*, 1857.

CHAPTER XIV.

FROM a letter received from Chuprah we have the following intelligence, dated 30th September. It will be seen that though the Rajahs were, as the correspondent writes, unequal to Mahomed Hossein in strength, they were not wanting in zeal or devotion. We must look more to intentions than to effects, and it is sufficient for our purpose that good feeling for the British Government predominated among the greater and best part of the population, and that that feeling was not unfrequently put to active demonstration, though under considerable difficulties and sometimes to positive disadvantage :—

"To-day I believe the Nogowlee Rajah marches to join his forces with the Gopalpore Rajah, when, with about 10,000 men, they go to attack Mahomed Hussien in Gorruckpur ; but with their undisciplined troops I fear they will not have much chance against the Oude people, especially if they have any irregular Cavalry with them, which reports of spies say, some 40 or 50,000 ; and if these Rajahs get licked, they will be worse off than before, as Mahomed Hussien will then send out troops to attack their houses and we shall have the rebels close enough to us. The Tumkoi Rajah had a visit from the Puddrora Tossildar. He was ready with the Baboos to attack him; but as he had only 40 peons with him and was civil, they let him alone. Young Nicholson writes, that the Bansee Rajah had been severely reprimanded by Mahomed Hussien for having assisted the Saheb-logues to get away, and a hurkura of the Bansee Rajah came to Nicholson, and told him the Rajah had written to him of his danger, that he had better leave the district for a while, but that this letter had been intercepted by Mahomed Hussien; this Mahomed Hussien also wrote to the Tumkoi man to know why he allowed a Saheb to remain in his Elaka? The Rajah replied the Saheb was doing no harm and was merely a *ghrihust*, collecting in his crops, altogether the Tumkoi man has taken every care of Nicholson and Bubnowlee."—*Englishman*, *6th October*, 1857.

A writer from Jubbulpore, says :—

"I forget now if I told you in my last that Dumah had been made to the care of the Punnah Rajah, who is faithful to our Government and has ample resources for proving a most worthy ally."—*Ibid.*

The following is from the narrative of the escape of an officer, dated Erinpoorah, 29th August :—

"A few Sepoys also covered me with their pieces, I called out, what, are you all against me? Then some troopers rose up, and got round my horse, and I took refuge in the Wurdu Major's house, and immediately sent off the two serjeants, who with their wives and five children, were foolishly attempting an escape on foot. Three Resildars, about forty troopers, now swore to protect or fall with me and I could have at this moment ridden off, but could not leave the wretched women and children, about whom no one seemed to care.

On the third day as I have said they marched, the cavalry riding round me, I had the satisfaction of seeing the women, Serjeants and children safely in the hands of a Vakeel of the Rajah.

From Abboo the people have been most kind, sending me clothes, tobacco, and so on.

The name of the Resildar who saved me, is Abbas Ali, and I hope he may escape. I have written to the General Commanding and Political Agent in Marwarra, to try and save this brave man, he is in danger, and is almost a prisoner, but having a strong party in the cavalry, they can't do him any harm, without injuring their own cause."—*Ibid.*

The following is an extract from a letter from Rewah, dated 27th September :—

"As I wrote you, an incipient rebellion took place when the force was moving to attack the first lot of mutineers. An express was sent to the Rajah to come, telling him that by his following our Agent's advice, it might be nipped in the bud. The officers were withdrawn from the force, that they might not be mixed up with internal dissensions, unless their services were applied for by the Rajah. Out came the Rajah and notwithstanding great opposition from his bad advisers, and we soon had things square. The Rajah then went to Jahajee, re-collected the force, inspected it, saw it march down the Ghauts and then returned to Rewah."—*Englishman*, 14*th September*, 1857.

The following is from Bubnoulee, 50 miles west of Gorruckpore, dated 7th October :—

"The Rajahs of Gopalpore, Sudasee, Bansee, Mujhoulee, and Tumkhoome constitute a Punchait. They are ready and willing to drive out the Chuckledar, but require British bayonets to lead the way, and inspire confidence.

I am, you will observe, nigh the scene of action being only 50 miles west of Goruckpore, but as yet I have not quitted my post for a day, and have been enabled to keep my own, owing, in no small degree, to the good feeling existing between the factory zemindars and the staunch and loyal behaviour of Kunj Bahadur, the Rajah of

Sumphoo, who deserves every praise for the measures he has hitherto taken, to preserve order in his Elaka."—*Englishman, 15th October, 1857.*

The following is from a narrative of an escape from Delhi :—

" About midnight the Rajah of Bullubghur came down and told as 50 sowars were after us, and advised us to change our clothes with our servants and get on to his fort as soon as we could, and he would try to protect us, whilst he went down and made all quiet. He sent a sowar out to meet us near the fort, and after waiting some time he returned, and we galloped into the fort, and were concealed ; immediately after, down came some 50 sowars at a hard gallop, who were told we had gone on ; they then dashed on, and we after a nap were sent on to a village, about six miles, in bullock carts used by women escorted by the Rajah's brother-in-law, where we remained five days in a small room at the top of the house, with only one small window and door. We started at night on camels, sent by the Rajah of Bullubghur under charge of a faithful man. We went down by the side of the Muttra road, passing around all the villages, until we came to the village of Euran, when our Camel-driver drove to the front and took us into the village, which we found blockaded by a cart and were obliged to turn back; four got out safe, but we with Mr. Ben, remained behind.

I got up and staggered off, very weak from loss of blood; I this time took another road and came on a party of armed men who conversed together, when they made signs for me to be off, and one offered to take me to a well to get water and was very kind in trying to pick a clear path for my shoeless feet and help me along.

Two villagers then came up and told me that two Sahib logues were gone to the next village, they gave me some water at a threshing station and showed me into the village when I found Messrs. Spencer and Cummings unhurt; the former kindly watched my wounds. They had fiered the head man 500 rupees each to take them to Agra. After a long parley he refused to take them, but took their guns and 300 rupees. We then received a note from Mr. Michell to follow the messenger and join him at a friendly village, two miles off, where he remained till evening, when our guide said it would be better to go on six miles further to a large village able to protect us, and they did for eight or nine days, though threatened by Marattahs with an attack.

P. S.—Michell obtained from the Rajah of Bullubghur all the horses except one and the loan of two hundred rupees, before we left Hadul, which was a great assistance."—*Mofussilite*, September 19th, 1857, quoted by the *Englishman*.

It is impossible to overestimate this service, but this Rajah being suspected of subsequent misconduct, was most brutally hanged. The State trials consequent to the Indian mutiny have few parallels in history for vindictiveness and hasty judgment. An European correspondent of the *Englishman*, compares the Punjab Officials to the Dantons and Robspierres of the memorable French Revolution, and says that the cruelties committed by them on pretence of the revolt, do not fall short o the horrors of the ignobly famous Black Hole of Serajooddowlah.* But whatever may be the character of the Punjab Officials, they do not surpass the North-West Officials in this respect. The single instance of the Rajah of Bullubghur sufficiently distinguishes their disposition and doings. If others have the glory of recommending the policy of repression and coercion, they can not match the glory of those who stamped their peculiar genius upon its execution. Assurances have been

---

* The details of the Punjab Black Hole will be given in a subsequent page.

repeatedly put forth that the protection of a single European would counter-balance all subsequent sins of omission and commission, but in the face of these assurances and in the presence of stubborn facts of aid and protection offered by the Rajah of Bullubghur, he was not deemed by the North-West Officials worthy of pardon or of a punishment lighter than that of beheading. The future historian will not fail to see that his blood rests on the head of his judges. And we can scarcely conceive what posterity will think of the policy practised at such an emergency towards people, who, whatever their subsequent conduct, will be known in history as saviours of Europeans. This serves to only embitter their affections, and deepen the difference of race.

The following is from Bhagulpore, dated 18th instant :—

"Lieutenant Rennie was saved by two Havildars, who brought him into Bhagulpore in a native marriage *dooly* which they hired, one man having forty rupees about his person. Poor Rennie was so overpowered from fatigue and hunger, that he could scarcely crawl, he had wonderful escapes, as the shots were flying in all directions.

"Mr. Gregor Grant was two days without food, on the third day he got to a village where they gave him some parched gram, *ookrah moree* and milk, he was very thankful for that. Shortly after he had been there, he heard that his kidmutghar was hiding in the village; he sent for him, and they got a *dooly*, as poor G. was unable to walk, having a large bit of flesh taken off the sole of his foot, he had only his night clothes, no shoes, or socks, in fact what he had on was only left to him. He lost his fine horse and elephant, his clothes, &c., were burnt, but all those things were nothing compared to his life being saved. He travelled in a covered *dooly* as his kidmutghar's wife, and came by a circuitous route; at the villages they heard the head-quarters also mutinied, and killed some officers, so he says, he was in a dreadful state of mind, fearing he would be killed if caught, but he got into the station all safe, through the interposition of a kind Providence."—*Englishman*, 23*rd October*, 1857.

Here is an instance of right feeling for a right object :—

"The residents of Bhaugulpore have subscribed eight hundred Rupees to Havildars Daria Singh and Thakoor Dhobey of the 32d Native Infantry for saving the life of their Officer, Lieutenant Rennie, when the detachment of the Regiment at Deoghur broke out into mutiny."—*Englishman, 4th November*, 1857.

Extract from a letter from Mr. J. W. Sherer, dated Cawnpore, 3rd November, supplied by Government :—

" The Gwalior contingent, to the best of my information, have not advanced beyond Jaloun. The main body of the defeated (in the Futtehpore affair), passed through the Ghatunpore Purgunnah to-day, but through the firmness of Beharry Singh and others, to whom I have made over the Purgunnah, they were not permitted to commit outrages, and indeed whenever they straggled in small bodies, were themselves attacked."—*Englishman, 10th Nov.*, 1857.

CHAPTER XV.

THE following is the petition of the Rajah of Wunurputty, volunteering his services and men in aid of the British Government for the suppression of the Mutiny :—

"TO THE RIGHT HONORABLE THE GOVERNOR-GENERAL OF INDIA IN COUNCIL."

&c., &c., &c.

MAY IT PLEASE YOUR LORDSHIP,

I the undersigned Rajah of Wunurputty, beg most respectfully to approach your Lordship with this humble address, earnestly hoping that it may meet with your favorable consideration.

With the deepest anxiety and horror have I heard and read of the barbarous and atrocious deeds of the mutineers of the Bengal Presidency and their cold blooded and deliberate proceedings are of such a nature as to stamp them with infamy and brutality unknown in the histories of the most savage and uncivilized nations. Hence my sympathies towards the British have been roused, and my wrath against the rebels has been kindled; so that if the offer herein made is accepted, I am resolved to revenge the atrocities committed on the subjects of the Crown of England with an unsparing hand.

I beg to assure your Lordship in Council of my loyalty, affection and attachment to the British Government, to whose kind and paternal protection I owe my life, my liberty, my safety and my all, and it would be disloyal in me not to tender my services at this painful crisis to aid in quelling the disturbances and in destroying and dispelling the mutineers. On a former occasion I proposed to go to the Crimea with a force to join the allied armies against the Russians, but the proposal was declined by Lord Dalhousie, on the score that the force was ample, and that my services were then not required. Permit me to refer your Lordship in Council to the Governor-General's letter No. 122 dated Ootacamund, 21st April, 1856.

With all due submission I take the liberty to intimate to your Lordship in Council, that I am resolved and prepared to start and join the English Army before Delhi, where the mutiny is concentrated, and to bring with me two complete Regiments of Infantry, one of Cavalry, and one Company of Artillery, which shall form a brigade under my command. I am well aware that my presence will unquestionably inspire the men with valour and confidence not easily to be shaken or intimidated. The body I intend raising, shall consist chiefly of Hindoos of my country, Seiks, Beloochees, &c. If your Lordship in Council should be pleased to acquiesce in the proposal now offered, I beg that the necessary instructions may be forthwith issued to the British Authorities, to afford me all the facilities I need towards the achievement of my design, and that preparations be made for the embarkation of my troops with the least practicable delay.

It may not be irrelevant here to inform you

Lordship, that the country of Wunurputty and its dependencies in the Hyderabad, Deccan, were held by ancestral and hereditary right and succession for nearly six centuries and that since the treaty between His Highness the Nizam's Government and that of the British, the country has been more firmly established and greater security has been extended to life, property and freedom throughout my country. It is a source of unbounded joy and gratification to learn that the friendship, alliance and good feeling existing between the English and H. H. the Nizam have been unshaken and undisturbed, and the series of years that has revolved, tends incontestably to prove that the object of the treaty has been realized, matured and confirmed. H. H. the present Nizam, H. E. Salar Jung Bahadur, the Dewan than whom the State has never had a more equitable and able Minister, and all the leading noblemen of Hyderabad Deccan, are well affected towards the British Rule in India, and are deeply interested in their welfare, success and prosperity. They view with disgust and abhorrence the conduct and proceedings of the rebels, and can in no manner justify them from whatever cause they may have originated. I can speak from experience, that when required, the Hyderabad, Deccan, is ready to put forth its colossal power in action against the insurgents and to crush the very name of Mutiny.

In concluding this address I beg to assure your Lordship in Council, that we Hindoos and all the British Subjects in the Hyderabad Deccan, are deeply indebted to Colonel Davidson, British Resident, for the security of our lives, property and persons, owing solely and chiefly to his unwearied exertions and to the timely and suitable preparations he has made to meet any outbreak or rising, and we repose the utmost confidence in his judgment and prudence, and in all the plans and measures he has been pleased to adopt at this dreadful and critical juncture.

With sentiments of respectful submission, &c., &c., *Englishman, 20th November*, 1857.]

No. 4282.

From

G. F. EDMONSTONE, ESQUIRE,
Secretary to the Government of India,

To

HIS HIGHNESS W. RAMASWAR BULVENT BHYREE BAHADUR,
Rajah of Wunurputty,
Dated Fort William, 21st October, 1857.

SIR,

I have received and laid before the Right Honorable the Governor-General in Council, your letter to the address of his Lordship, dated the 12th ultimo, praying to be allowed to render the British Government some Military aid in quelling the present insurrection in its dominions.

2. In reply I am directed to acquaint you that, His Lordship in Council feels assured that your Highness's troops would, if called into the field do excellent service. But the retaking of D lhi, and the arrangements that have been made for punishing the mutineers in all directions; renders it unnecessary for the Government to accept the aid of your troops. The Governor-G-neral in Council desires me, however, to express to you the thanks of the Government for your offers, and its approbation of your feelings of loyalty, and attachment to it.

I have the honor to be,

Sir,

Your most obedient Servant.

(Sd.) G. F. EDMONSTONE,

Secretary to the Government of India,

Englishman, 15*th Dec.,* 1857.]

In reading the above correspondence we feel a thrill of pleasure matched only by the importance of the subject. Here is a Native Prince, with an ancestry of six centuries antiquity, and master of a principality in the heart of Central India Proper, volunteering his services with an earnestness, the very expression of which was a source of comfort, not to say strength, to the British Government when many other Native Potentates were in a doubtful neutrality. We scarcely remember having read an Oriental composition breathing such enlightened feelings and sentiments as the volunteering letter of the Rajah Wunurputty. Government must have had good reasons for declining the offer. One of the reasons which Mr. Secretary Edmonstone assigns, is the circumstance of the recapture of Delhi, but the important reason which influenced the mind of the Governor-General was perhaps the rumour of an uneasy feeling about the tranquility of Hyderabad. Be it what it may, the good and earnest feeling of the Rajah was decidedly a great thing. We believe that similar letters have also been addressed to Government by other princes with the same object. We may say that imperial Rome was not more lamented and sympathized with by her dependant princes at the hour of her decline and fall than has Great Britain been during the Sepoy revolution. If the termination of this struggle had been different from what it is, we think the British nation would have had this pride that their fate like that of the glorious Romans was universally lamented by Asiatic princes and people alike.

CHAPTER XVI.

THE following is a brief account of the services rendered by the Rajah of Benares :—

"And it seems as unnecessary for me to give proofs of the Rajah's undoubted loyalty, for which he received a letter of thanks from the Governor-General. What few troops and armed men he has, have all along from the beginning of the disturbances, been at the service of the authorities; numbers of whom have been, and I believe still are employed at the Kotwallee, the thannahs and other places. He has done his best to prevent the mutineers from passing through his districts. His elephants, camels, horses, boats &c., have been at the entire disposal of Government, he has given supplies, his two large houses, called the New Mint, have been occupied since May by British troops and others, for which he neither has received nor intends to receive any remuneration. And he has lately lent another large house, rent-free for Government purposes, formerly occupied by the late Major Stewart, Agent to the Governor-General.

I think now, Sir, that you and your readers will agree with me, that, while others talk a great deal of loyalty, His Highness the Rajah of Benares has given proofs of it ; and that all attempts to impugn his loyalty are futile and absurd.

P. S.—It may be well to add that in August the Rajah received a proclamation from Kower Singh, stating that the King of Delhi had arrived at Agra or Allahabad with a large army, and that the Rajah of Benares had joined him. The very next day after the receipt of this paper, the Rajah published another, entirely contradicting it, and calling upon all people to adhere to their allegiance to the English Government."—*Englishman, 25th November*, 1858.

Here is a noteworthy instance of fidelity, exhibited under the most trying circumstances:—

"A trooper, named Sunker Singh, who has been invalided and was a private servant of mine, came running to me from the cavalry lines and said that the Sepoys of the 29th Native Infantry had mutinied and were firing on their officers. On my telling him that it was my intention to gallop to the Fort, he begged that I would not do so, as I would be killed by some of the men who occupied the only road (in the station) to the Fort, but he said that he would again ride to the lines and see what was going on. This he did, and on his return told me that the Sepoys were murdering the officers of their respective regiments all of whom had been in the lines, until the moment of the mutiny. He remarked, as they were killing all the officers, I had better conceal myself somewhere and on my suggesting my garden, he accompanied me there, and I was followed by all the women and children belonging to the servants of my establishment, and joined by my native Doctor and his family and some servants belonging to officers whose premises adjoined mine. We remained in the Garden until the guns of Captain Hungerford battery opened upon the mutineers with grape and canister. At the report of the second gun, the whole body of mutineers took to flight across the Race Course at the back or to the westward of the Dak Bungalow. When this occurred, Sunker Singh and some of my servants came to me in the garden and told me all that the mutineers had run away to Indore, and that I might return to the bungalow and sleep there with safety. I immediately proceeded with the rest of the people in the garden towards the bungalow, where I was stopped by one of my servants saying that he saw some Troopers at my doorway; on this, I again retreated to the garden and had been there about fifteen minutes when one of my servants came from the bungalow, saying, that there were eight troopers there and that they wanted some valuable native swords, knives and daggers which I had been collecting for many years: the whole of these they took, and two suits of chain armour with headpiece and gauntlets complete, and a second time they sent to me in the garden to say that they wanted some money: they took 800 Rs. cash, broke open boxes containing my full dress and undress uniform, and several silver cups and other large and valuable pieces of silver plate, presents from friends, some on account of professional services rendered; and others, souvenirs of friendship. The troopers deprived me of these, and six valuable horses, two pairs of bullocks, cows, goats and a four-wheeled waggon to carry the spoil: they threatened some of the syces and cajoled the rest, making them believe that I was dead: four of my sweesteters carried 7 of my dogs and were with the rest of the servants who decamped, very active in robbing me. After my servant had made his second visit to me in the garden I concluded that the troopers must know that I was close at hand, as their wishes were so immediately complied with, and considering myself not safe I left this place of concealment, followed by all the people that were with me; the Native Doctor and his family went to the Hospital and the rest scattered themselves in different directions: I came suddenly on two mounted troopers after leaving the garden, and hid myself in a drain and remained there the whole night. At day-dawn I again got into my garden, and lay down in the hedge nearest to my Bungalow; here I saw troopers in uniform riding about and 4 syces and grass-cutters on their tattoos going on the Indore road until about seven o'clock A. M. I also saw the two regimental standards carried off by two men of the 3rd troop on grey horses. My Mallee and Chokeydar became acquainted with my place of concealment and assisted me materially; and the wife of one of my syces, who also became aware of my being alive, went towards the Fort for assistance and fell in with the party of officers and the men of the artillery who had come out to seek for the bodies of the missing officers, they did not expect to find me alive, but on discovering me they carried me with the bodies of the three murdered officers to the Fort."

It was most gratifying to me to perceive the general satisfaction that my safe return produced. The European Artillerymen received me at the gate of the Fort with an unanimous "Hurrah," influenced by some little kindness I had shewn the Company at Cawnpore in 1853. As my Bungalow was so far from the Fort and no one to protect it, I was robbed of every thing by the villagers and the people in the Bazar. I have not recovered a single suit of clothes; every article of dress has been carried off, and every article of use either destroyed or taken away.;. I was dependent on my friends in the Fort for a change of linen for the first month of my residence in the Fort."

H. J. THORNTON, SURGEON,

1st Regiment, Bengal Light Cavalry.

Mhow, 20th October, 1857.

Englishman, 21st November, 1857.]

The Revd. Mr. Long kindly gave us the two following instances which occurred to him while on a conversation with us on this subject :—

"A young lad, employed on the Telegraph line in Benares, on the day of the Mutiny, was not aware of the state of things till he heard the noise of sepoys rushing into the compound and calling out for the Saheb; on this his syce seized him, thrust him under a heap of dung in the stable and told the mutineers the Saheb was gone away."

"An Ayah of a Futtyghur Civilian allowed herself to be cut to pieces rather than give up the Civilian's baby when demanded by the mutineers.

The following touching passages are

from the narrative of an eye-witness of the mutiny at Allahabad :—

"In the morning I got to the Bungalow, and found most of my people absent and the horse and buggy also, but a Rajpoot peon and two chokeydars were present, who helped to hide me in a fowl house. I was now getting weak from hunger, and I think delirious or mad, I don't know which, and during the Thursday afternoon, hearing some footsteps among the men of the bungalow, I ran out and saw one old Mussulman I ran up to him, got hold of him, and breaking off one of my shirt-studs, gave it to him, and told him to go to the village close by and tell my syce, naming him, that his master wanted his horse, and promised him the other two, and some besides, if he did so. I thought that if my syce heard that I was alive he would devise some plan to help me. But after the man had gone, I dreaded that he would perhaps play me false, and bring some of his cursed countrymen to punish me, so I went out at dark and crept along the hedges till I got into the stables of a neighbouring bungalow, and stopped there, awoke nearly the whole night, expecting a relief, but it came not and about day-light I fell asleep. I fancy it was about 7 o'clock on Friday morning, when I was awoke by some noise, and looking up, found three men standing over me with lattees. I now gave up all for lost. I was so weak I could hardly raise myself on my elbow as I lay on the ground. I looked at them and then told them, if they had come to kill me, to do so at once, and make an end of it. But it seems my syce had either seen the man the day before or heard him talking in the village, and dropped some hints to these men who, though all servants of Sahebs were all professional dacoits. Directly they mentioned the syce's name, I forgot hunger, fear, and all, and begged them to give me some food and a disguise to go into the Fort; offering them one hundred rupees each. They agreed to this course, brought me some food (which tasted deliciously,) and a lot of dirty old blanket which I was obliged to wrap all round me, and cover my head, to conceal my white skin, as well as white clothes, and then with a basket on my head, to help the disguise, I trudged away on Friday night to their village."—*Ibid.*

The following is from a letter from Simlah :—

"Though no lover of the Moslem, I cannot refrain from making known the promotion of our Kotwal, Wuzeer Khan, to the Kotwalship of his native city, Delhi. He is a man well known to the residents and visitors of the last 10 years, for his urbanity of nature and civility without obsequiousness, to the European community. He has had a meritorious rise from that of Chuprassee to his present position, and for his good conduct, has, on more than one occasion, deservedly received marks of approbation from several of his superiors, in the shape of handsome presents. His tact was eminently displayed during our panic, his promotion, though a loss to Simlah, is still gratifying to those who wish him well."—*Englishman*, 1*st December*, 1857.

CHAPTER XVII.

THE subjoined is a copy of a statement, made by the Moonsiff of the suburbs of Bareilly, relative to the massacre of Mr. Robert, Judge of Bareilly, Dr. Hay, and Deputy Collector Orr. It is a brief narrative of the outbreak of which it treats. The perusal of it will excite in the reader a painful interest, but we think it is impossible to suppress the sense of gratitude and admiration invoked by the heroic and devoted exertion of the Moonsiff :—

"I was sitting in my house, getting mselfsy

shaved when Mr. Robertson came to me, and in a state of much excitement, told me that the Native Infantry Regiments were in open mutiny. That Major General Sibbald and several other officers were murdered, that the Sepoys were setting fire to the Officer's Bungalows and destroying the public buildings, that they had liberated the prisoners, and that they were ransacking the treasury:—That he had heard the Native Infantry Regiments would march out of the Sudder Station so soon as they had taken all the treasure. That as the Irregular Cavalry was loyal, he thought peace and order would be soon restored through their assistance. In the meantime he asked to be allowed to remain in my house. I complied with his wishes, remarking at the same time that I was not aware of the mutiny, and candidly informed him that I had not sufficient men in my service to protect him, but that he was welcome to remain in my house as long as he liked. I had scarcely done speaking to this gentleman, when the two latter officers also came to me, and being curious to ascertain the nature of their errand, I asked Deputy Collector Orr what he wanted. I was told in reply that he had ordered his buggy to return certain visits, that his Kidmutgar came and told him that the Sepoys were in open mutiny and had murdered some of their officers; that they were taking the guns to knock down the jail and liberate the prisoners, that they would pass by the house, and for him to leave the house immediately, and he forthwith got into his buggy, and drove off to the Major General's Bungalow; that on his way he was informed that the Major General was killed, that he went then to the house of the Commissioner, and found that he had fled: that he then went off to the residence of the Collector, and found he had also fled with the Joint-Magistrate to Nynee Tal for refuge, that he next resolved to see Mr. Robertson, the Judge of Bareilly; that on his way he met Dr. Hay whom he took up into the buggy and both proceeded to the residence of Mr. Robertson, finding that the mutineers had preceded him he turned his buggy and put the horse in gallop, that the horse being frightened by the report of fire arms, became ungovernable and knocked against a tree and was much hurt, and that his buggy broke down; he heard that Mr. Robertson was in my house and so he wanted to see him. Shortly after this interview with the Judge Mr. Robertson desired me to send for the Kotwal of the city. I thought it an imprudent request, because it would lead to the discovery of their place of concealment. I remonstrated with him, but he repeated his orders; finding that he would not benefit by my advice, agreeably to his wishes I went up to my gateway, and seeing a Burkundaz of the Kotwallee standing there, I told him to call the Kotwal; in reply he told me that the Kotwal had concealed himself;

that Newab Khan and Bahadur Khan had come in person to the Kotwallee, and demanded the three gentlemen whom I had concealed in my house; that if I refused to comply with the Chief's request, he would put me to death and knock down my houses. I told the Burkundaz that I had concealed nobody; and he returned to the Kotwallee. On returning to the gentleman, I informed them of the messages brought to me by the Burkundaz of the Kotwallee from the Chief. They seemed to be much alarmed, and asked me to remove them into some other house. I could not do so, as all the city was up. Messrs. Hay and Orr resolved to go away, but the Judge Mr. Robertson, made up his mind to remain in my house at all hazards. To the two former gentlemen I folded my hands and begged of them not to expose themselves in the middle of the day in the streets of the city: they succumbed to my entreaty and made up their minds to stop in my house. As they appeared to be much frightened, I asked them to take refuge in my zenana, among the female members of my family; that they declined to do, stating that the zenana afforded them no greater security. However I concealed the Judge in a small room, giving him a small knife to protect himself in case his place of concealment should be discovered, and locked up the door. Messrs. Hay and Orr I concealed in another room, giving each of them a sword and pistol. I then locked up the gate and went off to the roof thereof. The budmashes now surrounded my house, and called upon me to deliver up the refugees into their custody. I swore to them by every thing that was sacred, that there were no Europeans concealed in my house. I was menaced and very offensive language was used towards me; they set to work with hatchets to break open the gate; but were foiled in their endeavours to do so. By means of a ladder they jumped into my brother's apartments; my brother resides in the same house with me. On seeing how they had effected an ingress, I came down from the roof to the gateway, and was unfortunately made a prisoner. By the same ladder they jumped into my house, and now commenced the bloody deeds, by a blow from a club I had a finger broken, and my toes bruised, the doors were burst open, the gentlemen dragged from their roofs and were most barbarously murdered by the Newab's emissaries. The guard placed over me, now released me and I saw the fiends carrying away the ladies of the deceased officers. I then went to the Kotwallee and asked them to bury the bodies. I was refused them by the Newab, who was greatly vexed with me, and made use of the most opprobrious terms which human ingenuity could devise. I then turned home, and found it was no longer a home for me. My property plundered, the female inmates of the house had fled for their lives, that my hardships are better conceived than described, and I trust to a generous Government to give me redress. In trying to save the life of my employer, I have lost my all and my losses are irreparable. The following residents of Bareilly, will bear testimony to the truthfulness of my statement, viz., the principal Sudder Ameen of Bareilly, Messrs. Brojonauth, Gooroodyal Khettree, the Sub-Assistant Surgeon of Bareilly, and Moonshee Nittanundo; besides several other Hindu citizens whose names it would be too tedious to mention, are eye-witnesses to the fact."—*Englishman, 2nd December*, 1857.

We should observe that the above statement has other merits than as a story of the personal sufferings of the narrator. The Moonsiff was a Government servant, and his influence as such, gave him considerable influence within his jurisdiction. The circumstances in which he was placed were also exceedingly tempting, and if he had displayed the least wavering or infirmity of mind, all would have been over —with British interests in that part of the country, and the rebels would have obtained in him a large accession of strength. But his moral courage swayed the chances that surrounded him. He not only presented a bold front to the insinuations and threats of the mutineers, but placed himself in the thick of the struggle by undertaking the protection of his European superiors and friends. He opened to them the zenana of his house, fed them, afforded them every shelter, and kept them informed of all the passing events. Though his exertions subsequently proved ineffectual, he spared nothing that could be of any use to them at the moment. To quote his own words; he lost his all for their safety; we hope with him, that a generous Government will give him redress.

CHAPTER XVIII.

THE following extract is from a letter, dated Noakhally, the 25th November:—

"Intelligence of the Mutiny was received in this station on the night of the 20th idem, and as the intended route of the mutineers was not then known here, our Magistrate, Mr. F. B. Simson, ere break of day, had nearly two thousand stalwart and brave men, armed to the teeth, ready for action, in case the mutineers paid us a visit; most of our men was supplied by the Bhulloah Rajahs, and the rest constituted the Jail and Treasury guards, the local battalion and the brave portion of the inhabitants of the stations—the few timorous ones having run away into the villages. Our little fortress was the Bhulloah Zemindary Cutcherry; a pucca building, encircled by strong brick walls; placed at the disposal of the Magistrate by Babu Jossoda Coomar Pyne, local Naib of Rajahs Pertaup Chunder and Issur Chunder Singh."—*Englishman, 3rd December*, 1857.

These Rajahs have their estates over all the Bengal Presidency, whether in the Upper or Lower Provinces, and have suffered in consequence of the mutinies perhaps more than any other Calcutta Zemindars. But wherever within their estates any disturbance took place, prompt aid was offered to the authorities there by their agents and servants. Government has more than once formally acknowledged their assistance, and we have lately read in the papers of one of their Naibs having been rewarded by Government for conspicuous exertions when the Government officers failed to mend matters.

"The Saugur rebels, with the mutineers 52nd B. N. I., lately attacked and looted Dumoah, releasing the prisoners from the Jail. A nephew of the Punna Rajah, with 12 guns and eight thousand men, some of them supplied by the Rewah Rajah, have advanced to take Saugur, but the Rajah of Saugur had fled to a Hill Fort, in the jungles, named Soorae, with four guns, so the natives say."—*Ibid.*

This sort of service is not rare in the history of Native exertions for the sustenance of British Supremacy. Natives, by scores voluntarily undertook to defend and keep places in the name of the Company Bahadoor though there were no representatives of the Government in the vicinity to give the necessary orders. We think this the more meritorious as the acts were entirely voluntary.

The following intelligence is extracted from a letter from Tipperah, expressive of the feeling that prevailed in that district on the receipt of an express from Chittagong, announcing the mutiny of the Sepoys there. It appears the express reached Tipperah on the night of Friday, the 20th instant, and created a general panic. The ladies and most of the gentlemen left the station without loss of time for Dacca, and the natives with their families to the villages on the opposite shores of the Goomtee River. The only gentlemen who continued in the district were Messrs. Metcalfe, Judge ; Sandford, Assistant to the Magistrate and Collector ; Barbar, uncovenanted Deputy Collector ; Martinelly, head clerk of the Judge's Court; Bruce, accountant to the Judge's Court. They were led to stay behind, it was generally understood, from a hope that in case of any disturbance, they would be assisted by the Maharajah's forces. There were also good grounds for this hope as the Rajah's men were kept in preparation for the purpose.

"On the morning of November the 30th, the Maharajah of Tipperah sent in a report, I presume to the Judge, to the effect that the mutineers who had entered his Hill Territory, were at Odoypore, and intended attacking Augurtollah, the seat of the Rajah. Should the mutineers put their intentions into execution, the Rajah's forces, joined by his Hill subjects, will, there is no doubt, soundly drub them."—*Englishman*, *9th Dec.*, 1857.

It appears that when the mutiny

Chittagong first broke out, the only fighting people that could be had, were those supplied by the Mooktagachee Zemindars. A Correspondent says :—

"He (Mr. Lance, the Magistrate,) was just at day before the panic began in the Mofussil, heard of it the same night and immediately arrived at the station to encourage the people. But with only some lattyals provided with some fire-arms from the Mooktagachee Zemindars."—*Englishman*, 14*th Dec.*, 1857.

A correspondent of the *Mofussilite* at Nagode, Central India, says :—

"A Sepoy of the 37th at Benares, took a letter from the Havildar of the 34th to the Rewah Rajah, offering the support of 2,000 men if he would rise against the English. The Rajah on the contrary, seized the Sepoy and sent him into Nagode where he is now under confinement."—*Phœnix*, 11*th May*, 1857.

These extracts are from a Government message :—

"The Putteewallah Rajah, and the Jheend Rajah, have sent troops and some guns to Kurnaul, there to join the 75th and 9th Lancers who were expected in Kurnaul yesterday."—*Phœnix, 18th May*, 1857.

"The Gwalior troops are marching there to assist the British troops."—*Ibid.*

The following relates about the measures adopted by the people of Meerut for the restoration of order on the breaking out of the insurrection :—

"A troop of cavalry, with a proclamation, were to go out on the 12th, yesterday, and another Contingent Rissalah, and strong body of Police, the first raised on the spot and the second strengthened with extra men, were to be sent out with volunteer (Canal) Officers and others to sweep the country round and check depredation. An old Afghan, named Jan Fishan Khan, was raising men, aided by the Deputy Collector and principal Sudder Ameen, and would soon give a good account of straggling scoundrels."—*Phœnix, May* 19, 1857.

The following is the intelligence received this day (date of extract) in Calcutta. It is of a very cheering nature :—

"Three Officers (names unknown) belonging to the Delhi Regiments, have been brought into

Meerut by a Syud who had protected them. Thirteen Europeans who had escaped from Delhi, had been protected by the Zemindars of a village near Bagput, and a troop of cavalry have been sent from Meerut to bring them in.

The Syuds and Jats in the neighbourhood of Meerut have declared themselves on the British side."—*Phœnix, May 20th*, 1857.

"Intelligence from Rohilcund is to the effect that the troops there are quiet, and that the Nawab of Rampore has written to the Magistrate, offering his horsemen for the service of the State."—*Phœnix, May 21st* ,1857.

The following is from one of the Telegraphic Messages, supplied by Government :—

"The Bhurtpore and Gwalior Rajahs are all sending their troops. Fifteen hundred horse and foot, with six guns, under Captain Munbee, Bombay Engineers, Captain Nixon, 25th Bombay, Native Infantry, Assistant Governor-General's Agent in Rajputana, and Mr. Young, Assistant Revenue Surveyor, have advanced from Bhurtpore. All the Chiefs and Rajahs around Delhi and in Rajputana, are shewing their fidelity, and will doubtless be rewarded."—*Ibid.*

"The apprehension of danger from the immense number of prisoners that made their escape from

Meerut are reported to be groundless, as the majority of those released jail-birds are said to be most anxious to return into custody, and only waiting to do so as soon as arrangements can be made for their reception. Some of the prisoners have actually returned, while many men have left their name and address with the Jailor and the Police, so that they may be informed at once 'when the Jail is ready for them.'" A better behaved set of prisoners it is impossible to conceive.

Here is a story about the Jhind Rajah :— "It is said that the King of Delhi sent some of the insurgents, Native Cavalry to the Rajah of Jhind, asking his assistance against the English :—the Rajah of Jhind happened to be outshooting or parading his regiment, and immediately he found out on what errand the cavalry had come, he turned round to his men and ordered them to cut down every man of them."

"The Rajah of Putteewallah, it is mentioned, has forwarded to the Commissioner all seditious letters that were sent to him."—*Phœnix*, 20*th May*, 1857.

The above paragraphs disclose facts which are the best demonstration of the feeling of fidelity which actuated the authors of those proceedings. These Princes are the representatives or heads of confideracies which were once the bitterest and strongest enemies of British Government. But with the position inverted, their feelings have assumed a character perfectly unexpected by the most sanguine minded. If however the friendship and good will of the Native Princes be historically interesting, the little romance of the Jail-birds will not fail to adorn a good many tales and to point their piquant morals.

CHAPTER XIX.

THE following is taken from a private letter, written by a lady, residing at Simlah, dated the 20th May :

"We are housed here in a comfortable little hut and are quite safe. We receive every kindness from the Rhana. Our party of refugees, besides ourselves, consists of eight ladies, five children and one gentleman."—*Phœnix*, *9th June*, 857.

The Bombay *Telegraph* and *Courier* gives the latest intelligence from Surat, which we subjoin :—

"The Maharajah has written to the Governor-General, placing the 3,000 horse of Baroda brigade and all his resources at our disposal, and he offers to head them."—*Phœnix*, 12*th June*, 1857.

A correspondent of the *Phœnix* writing from Benares, under date the 10th June 1857, says that he, with some of his friends, were indebted for their safety to a friendly Zemindar on the occurrence of the mutiny there.

The following intelligence was received from Government last evening:—

"The Rajah of Rewah has placed two guns and two hundred Sowars at the disposal of the Government for employment against the mutineers between Mirzapore and Rewah."—*Phœnix*, 17*th June*, 1857.

The following was issued as a *Gazette Extraordinary* :—

"The following report by Lieutenant DeKantzow, of the 9th Regiment N. I., on the good conwluct of some of the native officers and sepoys of the feelrps at the recent outbreak at Mynpooree, and the authoi issued thereon by the the Hon'ble Lieute-Princesovernor, North-Western Provinces, are pub-confideracgeneral information.

(Copy.)

Mynpooree, 26th May, 1857

SIR,

In compliance with the injunctions contained in His Honor the Lieutenant-Governor's letter of the 23rd, and in that of Captain Greathead, A.-D.-C. to His Honor, dated the 24th instant, I have the honor herewith to give the following account of those men of the late detachment of the 9th Regiment N. I., at this station, whose conduct I approve of during the late Mutiny, and to whom I venture to think, reward and promotion should, according to their respective merits, be granted; I also append a list of those unconnected with Mutiny, who were sick in hospital, or otherwise absent at the time the revolt took place.

1.—Sheikh Kadir Buksh (Kote Havildar of the 6th Company and Senior Havildar of the Regiment), was present throughout the whole affair, but refused to join the mutineers, I heard him refuse to join three distinct times, and he was in consequence obliged to leave for a village for safety. He joined me after the mutineers left, and has been with me ever since,

2—Ousan Sing (Kote Havildar, Light Company,) a most worthy and faithful man, protected me at the magazine and was the very last man to return to cantonment. He behaved nobly throughout, and I strongly recommend him to notice; his exertions in repressing the mutineers, and endeavours to save the magazine, endangered his life; and therefore, though much against his inclinations, ordered him to leave for safety.

3.—Noor Khan, Sepoy 6th Company, a most meritorious man, saved my life at the magazine, kept off the mutineers from attacking me when endeavouring to save the Treasury Room gate from being broken down: he behaved very gallantly during the whole affair, and gave me every assistance, I trust his services will meet with the notice they deserve.

4.—Ajoodiah Doobey, Sepoy 6th Company, I recommend this man as a faithful Sepoy and one who did his best to prevent bloodshed and the releasing of the Jail prisoners.

5.—Bullie Singh, Sepoy 3rd Company; one of those who remained with me during the whole affair, afforded me good service, and is a faithful and good man.

6.—Mukkhun Sing, Sepoy 6th Company; was on duty at the Post Office during the mutiny, but subsequently joined me, and has remained with me ever since.

7.—Khoosial Singh, Sepoy 6th Company; sick in hospital, when the mutiny took place.

8.—Khurrum Khan, Sepoy 6th Company ditto.

9.—Chadey, Sepoy 6th Company, was with the

mutineers, but refused to join them and has remained with me ever since.

10.—Chandey Chobey, Sepoy, 6th Company, ditto.

I have, &c.,

(Sd.) C. ADOLPHUS De KANTAZOW,

Lieutenant,

Late in charge 6th Company, 9th Regiment, Native Infantry."

With reference to the foregoing report and to the authority conferred by the General Order of the Right Honorable the Governor-General, No. 698 of the 19th instant, the Lieutenant-Governor, North-Western Provinces, was pleased to make the following promotions in the Native Army :—

"Seikh Kadir Buksh, Pay Havildar of the 5th Company, and senior Havildar of the 9th Regiment, to be a Subadar in the Army.

Orisan Singh, Pay Havildar of the Light Company, to be a Subadar in the Army.

Noor Khan, Sepoy of the 6th Company, is promoted to the rank of Havildar in the Army, and further is admitted to the order of merit. The promotion is given for gallantry, and the decoration for saving his Officer's life.

Ajoodia Dobey, Sepoy 6th Company; Bulie Singh, Sepoy 3rd Company, to be Havildars.

Chadie, Sepoy 6th Company, Chandry Chobey, Sepoy 6th Company, to be Naicks.

By order of the Hon'ble the Lieutenant-Governor of the North-Western Provinces.

(Sd.) C. B. THORNHILL,

Offg. Secy. to Govt., N. W. P."

Mofussilite, June 2nd 1857.

Phœnix, 28th June, 1857.]

Conspicuous as the above acts of loyalty were, rewards of them were equally prompt. But this only enhances the importance of the services. If other Officers and Europeans had come forth with the accounts of their deliverance and of Native fidelity as they saw it, we think the most sceptical would not then hesitate to attribute in some measure the safety of British India to the fidelity and exertions of the indigenous Indians.

The following from Meerut and Roorkee, dated 25th May, had reached the *Mofussilite* :—

"The Nawab of Sirdhana caught a spy from Delhi yesterday morning. He received intimation on Saturday evening, that such a person had come with several letters to different Mahomedan people in the city, calling on them to be prepared to join the Delhi insurgents on their arrival here, which would be very soon; the Nawab was all night searching for this man, and only succeeded in finding him in the morning after he had delivered all the letters but one, which, together with the spy, were immediately brought before the Military Authorities."—*Phœnix, 20th June*, 1857.

A Benares correspondent says, under date the 20th June:

"News has come that Lieutenant Tucker is in hiding somewhere in Oudh. A party of native volunteers (composed of rich natives only) have gone out to find him and bring him in."—*Phœnix, 24th June*, 1857.

The following was received from Government:

"At Hyderabad and Saugur, all was quiet on the 18th. At the former place on the 20th, a large number of Mahomedans had assembled at a mosque, and were dispersed by the Minister Salaar Jungh and his Arabs. Both he and the Nizam are staunch to the British Government."—*Phœnix 27th June*, 1857.

"A writer describing the mutiny of Juanpore, says that the Europeans were protected by a

Lalla of that place who took them to his own house and kept them in safety till the arrival of an escort. The party consisted of Messrs. Fane, Paske, Tuttle, Brynon, Unsworth, Reuther, Bradford and Julius Cœsar, and Mrs. Paske, Mrs. Reuther and children, Mrs. Cæsar and Miss Robinson."—*Phœnix, 3rd July*, 1857."

CHAPTER XX.

THE following reports and orders were published for general information in the *Government Gazette* of the North-Western Provinces, under date the 12th June, 1857 :—

"FROM

LIEUTENANT H. SWINHOE,

In charge of the late Detachment, 30th Regiment, N. I.,

TO

C. B. THORNHILL, ESQUIRE,

Officiating Secy. to Govt., N.-W. P.

SIR,

I have the honor to report for the information of His Honor the Lieutenant-Governor, North-Western Provinces, that the 7th Company, 30th

Regiment Native Infantry, under my command, mutinied on the morning of the 3rd instant.

2. It was reported by the Jemadar to me the 2nd instant, that some of the Sepoys exhibiting signs of discontent, I immediately went to the Sepoys on guard and asked them the cause of their discontent; they said that they had not received their pay for two months and were consequently unable to procure food.

3. I then went to the palace and petitioned the Rajah of Jeypore for the sum necessary for the payment of the Detachment under my command, for April. This request was graciously granted me, and the amount was distributed among the Sepoys.

4. I experienced great difficulty and even risk of life on entering the City Gates for the pay of the Company, on the afternoon of the 2nd instant, as orders had been issued by the Maharajah for the non-admittance of strangers. I applied for the pay of the Company at 5 P. M., and it was forwarded to the men at 9 o'clock that same evening.

5. As I was unable to obtain the pay of the Company until night I apprehended that were I to leave the Palace, I should not again obtain admittance during the night, should necessity require my so doing. I therefore determined to delay visiting the men till the following morning.

6. Early in the morning of the 3rd instant, Lieutenant H. Hawkins, 30th Regiment Native

Infantry, who was passing through Jeypore on his way to Nusseerabad, met the Jemadar of the 7th Company with a few Sepoys conversing with the native officer; he learnt that out of his guard, three Havildars, two Naicks, and 38 Sepoys had deserted him during the night. Lieutenant Hawkins urged upon those that were present to remain faithful to their posts. They asserted that they were willing to do so and expressed their utter unwillingness to join the mutineers. The above report was made to me personally by Lieutenant Hawkins on his gaining admittance into the palace.

7.—It was subsequently reported to me that 38 Sepoys had deserted with their arms and had proceeded towards Ajmere to join the insurgents, who, it was rumoured, were then within 12 miles of Jeypore.

8. I am happy to state the Jemadar is still present, and has with him one Havildar, 1 drummer and 18 Sepoys; he has also protected the stores and ammunition belonging to the Company, which were deposited in the Kote, from being carried away by the mutineers.

9. I have received every possible assistance and support from the Maharajah of Jeypore in procuring the books and papers belonging to the office at the Residency.

10. The conduct of the Jemadar Khoda Buksh Khan and the Sepoys who have remained by me,

I would wish to bring to the notice and favorable consideration of Government, to whom I venture to hope reward and promotion may be granted.

II. I have forwarded a copy of the above report to Colonel Campbell, commanding the late 30th Regiment Native Infantry, but as I am not confident of any communication reaching my Commanding Officer, I have thought it advisable to forward an account of those men of the late detachment 30th Native Infantry, who in no way took a part in the late mutiny.

I have, &c.,

(Signed) HENRY SWINHOE, *Lieutenant,*
In charge of the late detachment 30th Regt., N. I.

Ibid]

This Jemadar was promoted to the rank of Subadar.

"FROM A. O. HUME, ESQ.,
Offg. Magistrate, Etawah and others,

To C. B. THORNHILL, ESQ.,
Offg. Secy. to Government, N.-W. P.

SIR—As we find that the faithful and well-behaved men of the 9th Regiment N. I. at Mynpooree, have at once been reported for promotion to Government, we think it only fair to those of our Troops that remained true to us, under very trying circumstances, to do the same for them. We had intended to delay our report in regard to this matter, till peace was entirely restored, but to do so now, after the prompt acknowledgement of the services of the Mynpooreemen, would be an injustice to ours.

2nd—One Jemadar, two Havildars, one Naick, one Fifer, and 30 Sepoys (As by Appendix I) stuck by us from first to last. Of these the Jemadar Seodeen Sing Rajpoot was throughout conspicuous for his fidelity ; when at the first, many of the men, making paltry excuses of one kind and another, refused to march, and endeavoured to dissuade him from accompanying us, he said at once that, if he went alone, he would go, that he would never prove false to the oath he had sworn ; that they might kill him if they pleased, but go he would. This he said aloud in the presence of his officers, and manfully he bided by what he said. There are other good men amongst those who accompanied us no doubt ; but it is very questionable if more than half would have dared to remain true to us, but for the example set them by Seodeen Sing. When we were in the greatest difficulties and before we had received intelligence of reinforcement from Gwalior ; when, in fact, we had ceased to hope for any, and when the Natives totally disbelieved in the possibility of any coming (for Mr. Harvey had written on the 17th, that such were being sent, and we had announced it, and notwithstanding for six days further nothing had been heard of them) this Jemadar remained staunch and true, never presuming on our supposed weakness, and steadily promising of his own accord that come what might, he should remain faithful to his salt. We cannot praise this honorable Native officer too much and we sincerely trust that he may receive some marked reward.

3rd.—Hunnooman Sing and Nund Loll Tiwaree, Havildars, and Hunker Singh, Naick, are all deserving of great praise, being the only three out of eleven Non-Commissioned Officers of whose fidelity there could be no doubt. The men that remained with them withstood great temptation, and preferred the performance of their duty, under arduous circumstances and at a time when they really had no prospect of a reward, to the certainty of a share in the plunder of the Treasury.

4th.—The Duffadar of the detachment of the 7th Irregulars is another deserving man. It is really difficult to say which of the two men, Sheodeen Singh Jemadar, or Meer Hossein Ali Duffadar, behaved best throughout the whole affair. We cannot but feel that, with reference to the temper of the troops and the inhabitants of the district, that it was mainly the determined staunchness of these two men that preserved us from further injury. We proposed to nominate him Rissaldar of the new corps here, on a salary of Rs. 100, to commence with ; but he is deserving of something more. Of the 16 men under his command (See Appendix 2) Roshung Sing, Innayut Hossien, Nuthee Khan, Makhun Sing, are particularly deserving of honorable mention and promotion, though several of the rest also did fairly, and all openly at least remained true.

5th.—There are a few more with regard to whom we may hereafter have to report favorably, but of whose good conduct we cannot be certain without an enquiry into which, from circumstances already reported by the Magistrate, it is at present impossible to enter.

We have &c.,

(Sd.) A. O. HUME,
Officiating Magistrate,

(Sd.) H. R. CORFIELD,
Lieutenant.

(Sd.) C. D. R. ROSS, *Captain,*
Offg. Assist. Genl. Supdt.

Etawah, 4th June, 1857.

With reference to the foregoing report, and to the authority conferred by the General Order of the Right Honorable the Governor-General

No. 698, of the 19th May, 1857, the Lieutenant-Governor, North-Western Provinces, is pleased to make the following promotions :—

9th Regiment Native Infantry, Jemadar Sheodeen Singh, 4th Company, 9th Regiment N. I., to be a Subadar in the Army, and his name to be forwarded to the Supreme Government for the first vacancy for the honorable grade of Bahadoor.

Havildar Hunnooman Singh, 1st Company, and Havildar Nund Lall Tiwaree, 1st Company, to be Subadars in the Army.

8th Irregular Cavalry, Duffadar Meer Hossein Ally, 3rd Troop, to be Rissaldar; and Sowar Makhun Singh, 4th Troop to be Kote Duffadar; Sowar Roshum Singh, 4th Troop, to be Kote Ditto; Sowar Innayut Hossein, 3rd Troop, to be Kote Ditto, Sowar Nuthee Khan, 3rd Troop, to be Kote Ditto, in the Irregular Cavalry.

By order of the Hon'ble the Lieutenant-Governor, North-Western Provinces.

C. B. THORNHILL.

Officiating Secretary to Government, N.-W. P."

Ibid.]

CHAPTER XXI.

THE following is an extract of a letter from one of the sufferers in the neighbourhood of Azimghur, received *via* Ghazeepore :—

"On the night of the 3rd ultimo, the 17th N. I., in conjunction with the Sepoys that had arrived from Gorruckpore, mutinied, killed one of the Officers and wounded the Quarter Master Sergeant, released the prisoners from the Jail, helped themselves to all the treasure in the Collectorate, and then marched off with their booty towards Oudh, plundering and committing the greatest atrocities beyond any description. Whilst about sitting to breakfast at 11 A. M. of the following day, we had to run for our lives, leaving every thing untouched on the table, and in the hurry of the moment left behind three little bundles containing a few suits of clothes, &c., which had been kept in readiness in case of an emergency, as our servants had told us that the rebels were within sight, approaching our Bungalow. Mrs. ——— and Miss ——————— were supported on either side by our servants who dragged them to a village close by to prevent their falling into the hands of these wretches where we found refuge in the house of one of our Kidmutgars. Here we saw our property being carried off in all directions; after an hour or two, we were taken into another house which we were told would be more secure, but I suspect it was to prevent our seeing what was going on. Here we were locked into a wretched small place with two dirty charpoys and a gurrah of water. For three days and two nights we were in this miserable plight, with nothing but chuppaties to eat of which we took very little. They looted our Bungalow even to the very doors and hinges, and then set fire to it. They likewise burnt the factory and all that they could carry was taken away; the treasure chest containing 2,000 Rs. in cash was brought to a tope of trees close by our place of concealment, they endeavouring to break it open in which they failed. On the morning of the 3rd day after our flight, it was rumoured that we were to be murdered, but a kind Hindu by whose aid and protection, we set off to another village, saved us. On the following morning by his advice we went to a Rajpoot village, three miles further, where we were informed 2,000 Rajpoots would protect us from Mahomedan enemies. Here for 14 days we were pent up in a cowshed, living on such miserable food as was given us by our protectors, till the arrival of some elephants, twenty-two sowars and some matchlockmen sent to our rescue by the Commissioner from Benares."—*Phœnix*, 13*th June*, 1857.

Here is a noteworthy instance of loyal service. The Raja of Joypore has not only the credit of saving European lives, but of preserving order and tranquillity in the absence of all emblems of authority.

Camp Sonah, District Goorgaon, June 7th.

" Mr. Edward Hall, Mrs. Hall, Mrs. Barry and her three children have been released from a most painful residence amongst the Mewattees by the force of His Highness the Rajah of Joypore, commanded by Newab Fyz Ali Khan, accompanied by the Resident at the Joypore Court, Captain Eden in his political capacity. This force, consisting of Artillery, Cavalry and Infantry, is in every way well conducted and reflects credit on the state to which it belongs.

In our route yesterday from Jowrassee, we had a brush with the Mewattees, who showed an intention of impeding our march, they surrounded us on all sides, and it was found necessary to fire upon them, our men acted steadily and drove them back into the hills on our right. Our loss being two men and two horses wounded, that of the Mewattees is supposed to be about thirty men killed, it is to be hoped this example will do much good in chastising the marauding spirit in this district, the presence of the Maharajah's force has undoubtedly saved this town from pillage."—*Ibid.*

The following news reached Benares on the 10th instant :—

"All well at Gorruckpore, the Rajah of Gopalpore has assisted Mr. Pepper in destroying the bazaar of Muhadabar, where some of the refugees from Fyzabad were murdered."—*Phœnix, 22nd July*, 1857.

For the following items of intelligence from the Madras Presidency, we are indebted to the *Examiner* :—

"Our Correspondent at Mhow writes, on the 17th instant that all was safe there on that date, that Holkar was as staunch as ever and doing all he can to assist the authorities, but that he is in great danger himself as the few troops who have remained with him hitherto are not to be depended upon, especially since the return of some of the mutineers who are greatly incensed with him for his conduct in the outbreak. Intelligence had reached Mhow that the Bhopal Contingent which accompanied Colonel Durand and others to Sehore had mutinied and attempted a massacre of the survivors, who have been obliged to fly in all directions. Two officers and two ladies were taken prisoners by the Rajah of Jarah and were ordered to be put to death, but by the interference of Holkar were released, not without considerable trouble on his part and brought safe into Mhow about 9 o'clock on the night of the 16th instant; this circumstance places beyond doubt the fact that there has been a mutiny at Sehore, though our correspondent has not heard fuller particulars."—*Phœnix, 12th August*, 1857.

The following is an account of the exodus from Gorruckpore :—

"The station and all its property, &c., having been made over to the protection of the Rajah of Gopalpore, who has hitherto proved friendly to the English, the party crossed the Rabte and encamped for two or three days on its further bank, after which they moved forward towards Azimgurh."—*Phœnix, 27th August*, 1857.

The following intelligence was received from Government :—

"A party of the Dinapore rebels were reported to be proceeding westward (having passed south of Mirzapore) and Colonel Hinde, with the troops of the Rajah of Rewah, is supposed to be pursuing them."—*Phœnix, 27th August*, 1857.

"Our eccentric friend at Oolagunge," as the *Phœnix* has it, writes as follows, on Sunday, the 30th ultimo :—

"There was a strong talk, it is true, that the Rajah of Doomrao had been killed by Koar Singh, whom he tried to apprehend and place in Government hands. This is not the case, for I have since learned from, but why give up names? that the Rajah is still in the land of the living. He has retired to the interior of his district, to escape being captured by the rebels, who were of course, his enemies, for he was ready to assist Government, when his means failed him entirely."—*Phœnix, 4th September*, 1857.

Many are the conflicting opinions about the fidelity of the Rajah of Doomrao, but we are disposed to believe from all that has been written regarding this Rajah that he remained true to his allegiance, and that if he ever wavered in his conduct, it was more apparent than real. The communications of Patna and Behar "Newswriters" are so notoriously prejudiced and one-sided that they cannot command faith and even *they* are not unanimous about the bearing of the Rajah during the outbreak.

"Mr. Williams, the Commissioner of Meerut, has reported that the Hindoos of Bijnour had attacked and beaten the Newab of Nujeelabad and had petitioned for the return of the Civil Officers to their posts, adding that they were holding and would hold their country for the Sirkar against all comers."—*Phœnix*, 15*th September*, 1857.

We wish that all such facts had been reported to Government, or if reported had been communicated to the public to allay the fever of excitement which was brought on by inflammatory exaggerations and interested inventions of the non-official class.

While we are prepared to give every praise to British patriotism, energy, endurance, skill and bravery which have done so much to wrest British India from the iron grasp of the Sepoys, we still cannot blink the fact that all the resources of Great Britain, not to say of British India, would have availed little to crush the danger, had not the mass of the people rendered the most active and unflinching aid to the cause of order, and, where no assistance was offered, had not they remained singularly passive and to all appearances antagonistic to the revolt, and, what is equally important, did not the Native Princes. and Potentates continue unflinchingly faithful in their alliance and firm in their attachment.*

---

* In the last number of the *Quarterly Review*, there is an article on India, the authorship of which is generally atributed to the Neniveh Layard, the following passages occur :—

"It is principally to the fidelity and prudence of native princes and native statesmen that we owe the tranquillity of a great part of Central and of Southern India, as it is to the courage and faithfulness of two Sikh Chiefs, the Rajahs of Puttialla and of Jheend, that we owe the opportune aid of our first Sikh levies. Salar Jung, the Minister of the Nizam of the Dekhan, acting under the able guidance of Colonel Davidson, the Resident at the Court of Hyderabad, restrained, at the imminent risk of his own life, a fanatical Mahommedan population eager for Christian blood. The steady devotion of Scindia and Holkar left the Mahrattas without a leader of skill or influence, and has hitherto rendered harmless that formidable race."

"No one acquainted with the course of recent events, will be inclined to doubt that we owe the maintenance of our rule in India to the fidelity of certain of the Native Princes such as the Nizam of the Dekhan, Scindia, and Holkar, and the Rajah of Puttialla. Had either of them openly declared against us, no Englishman would probably have remained in the Peninsula. The Nizam would have carried with him the wavering populations of Southern and Central India, in either Scindia or Holkar the formidable Mahrattas would have found an hereditary chief of great influence, of youthful activity, and of no inconsiderable military abilities; the hostility of the Puttialla Rajah would have

CHAPTER XXII.

THOUGH the conduct of the British Government towards the Native States has been of late not very friendly or complaisant, and though against their independence and sovereignty sucessive Governors-General, excepting at some rare intervals, have been intently engaged, still the chiefs, with true instinct and faith, have firmly remained by the English even when the chances were clearly and indubitably against the British. It is notorious that these princes have been from the day of their connection with the British Government, subjected to a surveillance unknown in their history, which always barred the

---

left us without those Sikh allies, by whose aid alone we have been able to subdue the rebellion in the North. These four princes, the Rajpoot chiefs who have remained for the most part neutral or indifferent spectators of the struggle, and one or two petty Rajahs are the only native rulers to whom we have left any shadow of their former independence, or over whom the doom of annexation is not actually pending. We do not include Nepaul, which is scarcely an Indian state, although the result of a wise policy and friendiy relations with a native power have, in this instance, been remarkably illustrated."

development of their genius and policy, and the reins of which were relaxed only when particular Residents were open to pecuniary inducements or distinguished by a disposition which the higher civilization of Europe and enlightened international law ought to foster. They have had however the magnanimity to pass by the best opportunity that ever offered to avenge their grievances. They could have now easily retaliated their injuries and insults, practically demonstrated the *morale* of the annexation policy, which unfolded its terrible magnitude with the secession of every year and plucked the roots of their respective dynasties wider and wider, but no, their religious teachings and political convictions have directed them to a quite different course, contrary to the expectations of all political reasoners, but perfectly in keeping with the principles of Asiatic friendship. But the conduct of the Native allies were not simply neutral; were it such alone it would have been a tower of strength to the British Government. It was marked by as signal acts of assistance and protection as the emergency of the times required. "The Rajahs or Native Princes of the country," says the *Times*, "have shown a signal attachment to the British Government, and have supported promptly with their followers while the great land-holders themselves equivalent to the territorial lords, have without exception, been firm in their allegiance." Indeed if we take but a summary glance at the events of the last fifteen months, we shall find that there was scarcely a place saved or a victory won without some assistance in men, money or in provisions, of some neighbouring or distant Native potentate or some princely landowner. In the glory of the world-renowned triumph before Delhi which is said to have "broken the neck of the rebellion" the contingents of the Rajahs of Puttiallah and of Jheend had no mean share. Their fidelity, gallantry, and devotedness have been noticed in the highest terms of applause, both by Sir Archdale Wilson and by the Governor-General in Council. The services of Jan Jishan Khan and Sirdar Meer Khan Sahib on that important occasion, were also of a character which justly elicited the admiration of Lord Canning. The promptness and unswerving good-will of the Maharajah of Gwalior saved Agra in the most critical period of the crisis. The friendship of this Prince has been subsequently tried by the hardest test known, and he has, as our readers are aware, wonderfully well stood the fiery ordeal. The Rajah of Rewah, though not subjected to equal difficulties, has given numerous proofs of fidelity and attachment under circumstances each of which was calculated to deter a less determined and firm spirit. Both the Nizam and the Holkar have continued admirably steady in attachment and have framed their policy with a tact and wisdom equal to the importance of the times. The services of the Minister of the Goorkhas, whom an officer serving with the besieging army in Delhi, calls "the truest and bravest soldiers in the British army" are so well known that any elaborable delineation of them would be a work of super-erogation. But it is not only as friends, supporting the British with aid and influence, that the Native allies will be mentioned by the future historian. Their own domestic administration, in this universal crisis, will be a lasting monument of their administrative skill, genius and wisdom. Our readers are aware that the effects of the Sepoy revolution were felt in all the corners of India. The Native States experienced this shock the greatest. These contained the elements of rebellion and disorder in a condition ready to burst. Both the people and the contingents belonging to some of the principal Native States, from whatever cause we shall not wait to consider, were not well disposed to the British Government. Their sympathies with the Rebel cause were also forestalled by the ties of blood, birth, and religion with the Sepoys. Mr. George Campbell calls the Sepoy revolt a Hindustani movement, and the best illustration of this theory is met with in the state of feeling among the contingent troops of the Native princes. Hence Hyderabad was during all the anxious period of the crisis a burning volcano, ready to throw up its liquid lava at the least commotion. More than once it approached to convulsion, but the superior mind, energy, tact, and courage of Salar Jung, who has been justly characterized as the type of the educated natives, seconded by the friendly wishes of the Nizam and the Hydrabad Court generally, got over the crisis and restored the wonted calm. In *Chamber's Chronicle* of the Indian Revolt we find the following connected narrative of the position of affairs in the Nizam's territory :—

"The three Presidencies were all anxiously watching the state of feeling in the large and important country of Hyderabad, the dominions of the Nizam; for that country borders on Nagpore on the north-east, while on the south-east and on the west it is conterminous with districts belonging to Madras and to Bombay respectively. Its two largest cities, Hyderabad, in the south-east portion, and Aurungabad in the north-west, contained many English families belonging to Military and Civil Servants of the Company; or at least the families were at stations not far from those cities. By the terms of various treaties between the Nizam and the Company, the latter had the right of maintaining a large Military cantonment at Secunderabad a few miles north of Hyderabad city. This cantonment was three miles in length, and was well provided with officers bungalows and mess houses, European Barracks, Sepoy lines, Horse Artillery lines, Foot Artillery Barracks, Native Bazars, Parade ground, Hospitals, Arsenal, and all the other requisites for a large Military Station. The Cavalry lines are two miles north of the cantonment at Bowenpilly. The Military Station for the troops belonging to the Nizam, an independent Sovereign, was at Bolarum, somewhat further away from Hyderabad, but still within easy reach of Secunderabad. At the time of the Mutiny the British Resident at Hyderabad was placed in a position of some difficulty; At length there was collected a large force at Secunderabad, it comprised scarcely any British troops; and therefore, if trouble arose, he could only look to defence from natives by natives The capital of the Deccan, or the Nizam's territory comprised within itself many elements of insecurity. The government and a large portion of the inhabitants were Mahomedans, the rabble of the city was numerous and ruthless; the Nizam's own was formed on the same model as the contingents which had so generally mutinied in Hindustan; the Company's own forces, as just mentioned, were almost entirely native; and the city and province were at all times thronged with predatory bands of Rohillas, Affghans, Ables, and other mercenaries, in the pay of the nobles and other Jagheerdars of the Hyderabad Court. It is almost certain that if the Nizam had turned against us, Southern India would have been in a blaze of insurrection; but he was faithful and his Chief Minister Salaar Jung steadily supported him in all measures calculated to put down disturbance. The news of the rebel triumph at Delhi has set in tumult the turbulent Mossulmans of Hyderabad; and it has been all observed that a single moment of indecision, a. single act of impolicy, a single false step, or a single admission of weakness, might have turned Hyderabad into a Lucknow, and made a second Oude of Deccan. The Nizam, his Prime Minister and the British Resident, brought all sagacity and firmness to bear on the duties of their respective offices, and thus the Deccan and Southern India were saved. What might have been the case under other circumstances was foreshadowed by the events of the 17th July. On the preceding day, intelligence was received at the Residency, which stands clear of the city, but at the distance of some few miles from the British cantonment at Secunderabad, and the mob in the city was much excited, and that a scheme was on foot to press the Nizam to attack the Residency. Notice was sent from the Residency to Salaar Jung, and preparations were made. Early in the evening on the 17th, a Rohilla rabble stole forth from the city, and made for the Residency. An express was at once sent off to cantonments for aid; and in the meantime the guard, with three guns, and when Cavalry and Horse Artillery arrived at Secunderabad, the Rohillas received a total discomfiture. This was almost the only approach to a mutiny that occurred in the portion of the Deccan near the Carnatic frontier.

"Aurungabad on the Bombay sides of the Nizam's dominions, was, in regard to mutinies less important than Hyderabad, beoause more easily accessible for European troops; but more important in so far as the Sepoy Regiments of Malowah and Rajpootanah were nearer at hand to be affected by evil temptation. The city is about seventy miles distant from Ahmednuggur, and a hundred and seventy from Bombay. Uneasiness prevailed here so early as June. The first Cavalry and the 2nd Infantry of the Corps, called the Hyderabad Contingent, were stationed at Aurungabad, and of these the former shewed signs of disaffection: Captain Abbot commanding the Regiment, found on the morning of the 13th, that his men were murmuring and threatening, as if unwilling to act against mutineers elsewhere; indeed they had sworn to murder their officers if any attempt were made to employ them in that way. Fortunately the Rassaldars—each being a Native Captain of a troop of Cavalry, and there being therefore as many Rassaldars in a regiment as there were troops or companies, remained faithful; and

Captain Abbot with Lieutenant Dowker were enabled to discuss with these officers the state of the regiment. The Rassaldars assured the Captain that many of the troops had begun to talk loudly about the King of Delhi as their rightful ruler. The Resident at the Court of the Nizam, through the Military Secretary Major Briggs, advised Captain Abbot, seeing that no aid could be expected from any other quarter—to speak in as conciliatory a tone as possible to the men, and to promise them that they should not be required to act against the insurgents at Delhi, provided they would be obedient to other orders. Quiet was in this way restored, but it being a dangerous precedent thus to allow troops to decide where and against whom they would choose to fight. Major General Woodburn, who had been placed in command of a moveable column from Bombay, marched through Ahmednuggur to Aurungabad. This column consisted of the 28th Bombay Native Infantry, the 14th Dragoon, Captain Woolcombe's battery, and a pontoon train, when Woodburn arrived, he found that the ladies all left the Aurungabad Station, that the officers were being barricaded in the mess-room, and that all the Nizam's troops exhibited unfavorable symptoms. The first Native Cavalry when confronted with Woodburn's troops, behaved in a very daring way ; and about a hundred of them made off owing to the unwillingness of the general to open fire upon them, although Abbot and Woolcombe saw the importance of so doing.

"In the country North of Bombay and between it and Malwah many slight events occurred, sufficient to show that the Native troops were in an agitated state as if oscillating between the opposite principles of fidelity and treachery. It was worthy of note, however, that the troops thus affected were, in very few instances those belonging to the Company's Bombay Army; they were generally contingent corps, or Mahrattas or Rajputs, or men imbued with the same ideas as the Hindustanis and Oudians. Towards the close of July, a few troopers of the Gugerat irregular horse endeavoured to incite their companions to mutiny, they failed and then decamped; but were pursued and captured, and then hung in presence of their own Regiment."—*Chambers' Chronicle of the Indian Revolt.*

CHAPTER XXIII.

But the whole history of the Hyderabad crisis has been given in a well-written article in the *Friend of India* from which we quote the following passages:—

"All who were in India in May, June, and

July of 1857, recollect the intense anxiety with which our position at Hyderabad was viewed and watched. It was by far the most influential Native State in India, and there the Mahomedan element was known to be most powerfully predominant. The means of striking a deadly blow at our power, were not only present, but more united than elsewhere in India. It was not only that the population of Hyderabad estimated at 300,000 might at any moment rise, but that the movement might be aided by Arabs, Rohillas, Patans and other mercenaries, whose power had been known long before the rebellion, and who had always been closely watched by our own Government. The jealousy of our existence in India which was felt by those tribes, had often been openly manifested, and at any time was barely concealed. Would they resist such an opportunity as the rebellion in the North of India offered? Would the Hyderabad Contingent be safe? Might it not join, as other Contingents were joining, the general sedition? and if it did, was it not from its superior organization and power in Cavalry (the best in India), specially to be dreaded? If Hyderabad went, would not the Deccan—the Southern Mahratta country, and the Madras Presidency go too? That any disaffection, however slight, would have added immense complication to the general affairs of the period was but too evident. We had no European Troops with which the

Deccan could be reinforced: there were but two weak battalions of European Infantry in the Madras Presidency: and if disorganization had followed the events of May, or mutiny had broken out at Hyderabad, it is evident that it might have extended to the people of the Bombay and Madras Presidencies, and possibly, in a great measure, to the armies of both. Not a mail then arrived from England, in which there were not the most fearful anticipations of evil from Hyderabad: and who can say that they were light or unfounded? We, who weekly recorded the simple fact that Hyderabad was as yet safe, did so, we own, with deep misgivings, which we dared hardly to have expressed openly.

"In addition to the city, there were four large districts representing a population of upwards of three millions of people, which had been lately ceded to British management. The cession had been an unpalatable measure to the late Nizam, and it was an additional cause of dread therefore, as to whether the people would even continue to obey their few and sparsely scattered officers, and whether disturbances might not arise in them to distract attention, and impede that concentration of power which was needed elsewhere.

"Let us therefore review how these elements of profound danger were controlled: and how they were not only controlled, but changed in character; and eventually became, under the able guidance of one man, elements of positive strength to the British cause in India. The Punjab, a British province, administered by an English Officer of vigorous character, became, as we have already shewn, an active and powerful means of strength. Hyderabad could not be so entirely turned to account. It was a Native State and its physical resources were not available: but its partially active exertion, its entire tranquillity, and direct moral influence in our favor, constituted together an element of strength, which is entitled to its full meed of recognition and acknowledgment, and may stand fairly in its own degree, beside the more brilliant, though scarcely more vital aid derived from the Punjab.

"The conduct of this Court was the hinge on which the whole of the events South of the Nerbudda turned; and we may say now that the danger is past, that had a Jehad or holy war been proclaimed by the people, or by the head of the State: had the young sovereign been deluded by the Priests of his faith, or been dazzled by the prospect of enlarging his power for an hour, nothing could have averted that outbreak from Hyderabad, eastwards, westwards and to the south, the prospect and effect of which we have already contemplated.

"At an early period after the outbreak of the 10th May, and when it was apparent that a powerful rebellion was organized in Hindostan;

when Dehli had once more assumed importance as well from the position of the King as from temporary strength: when for a time, murder was successful to a degree hardly anticipated by the most sanguine of the Delhi party, when troops, treasure, and material of war were abundantly provided—it was clear that the Deccan largely sympathized with the movement, At Poona and Bombay, at Belgaum and Kolapoor, at Bangalore and Kurnool, as well as at Hyderabad, intrigue and sedition were actively busy: and the consequences of any contemporary success, anywhere within this area, would have been most momentous. It is true, that owing to the fearless bearing, the sagacity, and the precautions of Lord Elphinstone, the intrigues in the Bombay Presidency were crushed as they appeared; but his exertions, able and remarkable as they were, would have availed little, had the Hyderabad Durbar been avowedly hostile. We may briefly notice the chief local native authorities at Hyderabad on whose conduct events in a great degree hinged.

"Just as the rebellion commenced, the present Nizam Afzul-oo-Doolah ascended the Musnud. Hitherto, like all princes of his race, he had lived in the Zenana. He was utterly unversed in public affairs of any kind, and was known to be susceptible to the advice of intriguing Fakeers, precisely the classes from which the most dangerous counsel was to be apprehended. Europeans were personally unknown to him except by repute, which was perhaps unfavourable. His personal character was unknown, because untried, and his feelings and those qualities or impressions which his advisers could turn to loyal account, had to be ascertained, or were to be developed, by circumstances. Here therefore was no solid ground for action, or for supposing that he would withstand the temptations of the period, beyond an hereditary conviction that in alliance with Europeans lay the safety of his dominion.

Fortunately there were others on whom dependance could be placed. The Nizam's maternal grand-uncle Shumsh-ool-Oomra, an aged man, possessed influence with his nephew. His counsels now were to preserve good faith and amity with the British Government. They were exerted with the happiest effect, not only on the Nizam himself, but on the most bigotted and fanatical party in Hyderabad, of which, from religious motives, Shumsh-ool-Oomra was the ostensible and acknowledged head. It was fortunate too, that from a friendship of many years' duration, he had a high personal esteem and respect for the Resident Colonel Davidson; and this, by the Resident's tact, was admirably turned to account. Notwithstanding that disaffected persons thronged to his palace by day and night, and used threats, entreaties, and even imprecations to induce him to turn against the English cause,:—

notwithstanding that members of his own family were avowedly bitterly opposed to him in this crisis,—he never swerved: his answer to all was, "you know not what you are proposing: after an experience of more than fifty years, I tell you that there is no person in India that can resist the British power, nor does the Almighty render aid to those who massacre women and children. Formerly the men of Hindostan waged war only with men."

The Minister of the State was Salar Jung, a young man, well educated, whose sympathies by education, and we may perhaps add, interests also, were on the side of the British. For this position he was hated, nay execrated by the revolutionary and fanatical party. His assassination was meditated as an enemy to the State and to the Mussulman faith. Subtle intrigues were laid against his power, and in local affairs he was opposed by Shumsh-ool-Oomra and his sons. But in his line of conduct from first to last there was no wavering or tottering. The Jehad or holy war against infidels, was an object scarcely concealed by highly influential parties in the capital, and on several occasions was proclaimed by the rabble. At any time an impulse difficult to control, it was rendered doubly so by reports of the discomfiture, ruin, and massacre of the English in Hindostan which were proclaimed with insulting exultation. Thus sorely pressed, the Minister never flinched from his duty, or wavered in his truth. He held the Arabs with him, or a large section of them. With them he guarded the city, prevented tumultuous assemblies, and controlled the populace. Finding that open violence would not succeed, the disaffected conspired in secret, and the result was the outbreak and attack on the Residency of the 17th July, which if successful would have involved the destruction of the Minister as well as of the Resident.

It was thus by the firm conduct of two individuals of the Hyderabad nobility, that an outbreak of an universal character was averted. Had they been treacherous, or lukewarm in their course of conduct,—had both, in their several degrees of influence, not acted so as to shew the Nizam unmistakeably his true policy, had not both possessed commanding influence with the Arabs and other mercenaries, we cannot doubt that the attack of the 17th July would have only been the prelude to scenes like those of Cawnpore and Lucknow.

It boots not now to enquire whether the Native regular Troops at Hyderabad were then staunch or not. The impression was, that disaffection very strongly pervaded the whole of the subsidiary force, and only required a leader, or temporary success anywhere to break into open violence. There is no doubt they were actively canvassed and tempered with by emissaries of sedition,

On one occasion of a non-official visit to Shumsh-ool-Oomra by the Resident, men of the escort openly shouted to, and harangued the most dangerous and fanatic portion of the city populace then assembled at Shamsh-ool-Oomra's house. Emissaries from the city were busy in the Cantonments, and for a long time it seemed doubtful whether the troops would resist the corrupting influence so freely, and so constantly exercised. Can it be said, or hoped, they would have done so, had the Nizam and his nobles, the mercenaries and the Moulvies with their rabble risen *en masse*, and raised the Jehad and the country with it? We fear not. That an impression, false or true, prevailed that the Troops were *not* staunch; that the Resident's escort would fraternize with an *actual* movement, there seems little reason to doubt. Had this not been the case so small a force would never have attacked the Residency. The result undeceived the conspirators. The detachment on duty at the Residency under the command of Major Briggs was staunch, the local arrangements by that officer were excellent, and the attacking party of Rohillas, led by Toora Baz Khan, the most notorious ruffian of the Deccan, was repulsed by grape. Expècting assistance it was staggered by the cool reception it met with, and there was no further attempt at violence.

But apprehension did not cease here, on the

contrary, it was most probable as times wore on that this was only the prelude to a further and better organized attempt. Reports of successful atrocities in other places were frequent, nor had we as yet assumed any attitude, or begun any operations, suited to the emergency, or calculated to stem the tide of opinion against us. It was argued and with apparent truth, that the Nizam's Government might have prevented the attack had it chosen to do so: that the Minister and the Nizam could not, even if they desired it, control their own people and that the disaffected party in the city were stronger and bolder than before. Toora Baz Khan was apprehended and tried, but a decree of death could not be obtained against him, because he had undertaken a Jehad against Infidels! and he was not executed. All these were additional subjects for anxiety and apprehension.

* * * * *

The firm attitude of the Resident gave the Minister new heart. He brought up his own troops into the city in large numbers, and took up positions to overawe and crush any seditious disposition or attempt during the Mohurrum. These troops were faithful *because confidently directed*, and if there had been hope, or intention of insurrection, the opportunity was allowed to slip. The local arrangements in the cantonment were admirable—and the dreaded Mohurrum passed off even more quietly than usual.

Thus reviewing the whole course of local events from May till the fall of Delhi, we consider that the prevention of seditious outbreak at Hyderabad by the patient fortitude, political sagacity, and calm resolution of the Resident Colonel Davidson, ranks as high in the scale of eminent and useful service in the time of trial, as those more outwardly brilliant and apparently more noticeable actions in the field which fell to the lot of other officers. It will not do, now that, as we trust, all danger is past, to lessen the obligations attached to these services, by saying there was but trifling excitement at any time.

Nor would we be thought indifferent to the claims of these who so nobly and so disinterestedly seconded the efforts of the Resident. The Nizam, the Minister Salar Jung and Shumsh-ool-Oomra each in their several degrees deserve the grateful acknowledgment of their services, which we trust will be specially conveyed to them by the Queen herself. If there be any mode more cordial, more effective than another personal decoration, or in the Minister's ase guarantee of power, estates and office, for which we have many precedents, we shall gladly see it bestowed. In any case official silence, or cold indifference would be inexcusable."—*Friend of India.*

We are however not in a position to affirm the extent to which the courage, prudence and tact of the Political Resident contributed to the preservation of order and the quietting of the turbulent elements in Hyderabad. If we are to weigh in the scale the mass of proofs and reflections which almost the whole Madras Press has produced against Col. Davidson, with the glowing passages of the *Friend of India*, we should naturally qualify our opinion of the Resident. He may have displayed extraordinary courage, abilities, self-control and promptitude of thought and action, but where opinions are so conflicting and where there are no sufficient data before us, we cannot express a different judgment from what we have done. It is however exceedingly gratifying to observe that with regard to the noble feeling of the Nizam, the statesmanlike conduct of the Minister, and the friendly advices and exertions of Shumsh-ool-Omrah and other courtiers, there is but one opinion—*viz.*, that they have by their energy, decision, promptitude, and friendliness conducted Central India safe through a too imminent crisis which would have terminated with the dismemberment and desolation of the whole of Hindoostan.

CHAPTER XXIV.

WITH regard to Gwallior and Indore, the chronicler gives the following narrative :—

"Still further northward lies the country which, under the various names of Scindia's territory, Holkar's territory, Malwah, and Bhopaul, has already been described as the chief seat of the Mahratta power, and which corresponds pretty nearly with the region marked out by the Company's Officials as Central India. We have seen in former pages that Scindia, chief of the Mahratta State of which Gwallior is the capital, offered the aid of his Contingent army to Mr. Colvin, in May that Lieutenant Cockburn, with half a cavalry regiment of his Contingent, rendered good service in the region around Agra, until the troopers deserted him; that the fidelity of Scindia to the British alone prevented his troops generally from joining the rebels, for they belonged to the same Hindustani and Oudian families, though serving a Mahratta prince in a Mahratta State, that after certain detachments had mutinied at

Neemuch and elsewhere, the main body rose in revolt at Gwallior on the 14th of June, murdered some of the English officers, drove away the rest with their families, and formally threw off all allegiance to the Company, all that Maharajah Scindia, under circumstances of great difficulty and peril, managed to keep peace at Gwallior—retaining and feeding the troops at that place and yet the discountenancing the mutinous tendencies against the British. If he had not acted with much tact and judgment, the Gwallior Contingent would have marched to Agra in a body, and greatly imperilled the British Rajah. Not only did he keep those troublesome troops near him during the remaining half of June but also during July and August. Scindia's special army, entirely under his own control, were chiefly Mahrattas who had little sympathy with the soldiers of the Contingent; but they were too few in number to put down the latter, and therefore he was forced to temporise—partly by persuasions and promises—partly by threats. Major Macpherson, the British Political Agent, and Brigadier Ramsey, the Military Commandant, ceased to have influence at Gwallior, it was Scindia's good faith alone that stood the British in stead.

Holkar's Mahratta territory with Indore for its chief city, we have, in like manner, seen to be troubled with a mutinous spirit in the Contingent troops, partly owing to temptation from other quarters. We have briefly shewn in the chapters lately cited, that on the 28th of May, the 15th and 30th Bengal Native Infantry revolted at Nusseerabad, that on the 2nd June influenced by this pernicious example, the 72nd Bengal Native Infantry, the 7th Regiment of Gwallior Contingent Infantry, and the main body of the 1st Bengal Native Cavalry, mutinied at Neemuch, that on the 1st of July a portion of Holkar's Contingent rose against the British at Indore, without his wish or privity, and that he could not get even his own special troops to act against those of the Contingent; that on the evening of the same day, the 23rd Bengal Native Cavalry mutinied at Mhow; and that numerous British officers and families were thrown into great misery by these several occurrences. It now remains to be stated that during July and August, Holkar adopted, nearly the same course as Scindia, he remained faithful to the British, and endeavoured to quell the mutinous spirit among his troops. Holkar possessed, however, less influence than his brother-Chieftain; most of the mutineers from Indore and Mhow marched to Gwallior, and were only prevented by the shrewdness of Scindia, from extending their march to Agra.

Among the troops in Rajpootanah were the Deesa Field Brigade, commanded towards the close of August by Brigadier Creagh, who had under his control the troops at Deesa, those at the sanitarium on Mount Abboo, and those at Erinpoorah and other places in the neighbourhood. These places were thrown into confusion during the last two weeks of the month, by the mutiny of the Jodhpore legion, consisting partly of Cavalry and partly of Infantry. Such of these men as were stationed at Erinpoora about 550 in number, rose on mutiny on the 22nd. They suddenly threw off their allegiance, seized the guns, made prisoners of Lieutenant Conolly and the European Sergeants, plundered the bazar and some of the native villages, burned all the Officers' Bungalows, and destroyed or appropriated all that they found therein, lived in tents on the parade ground for three days' and then marched off in the direction of Nusserabad. The Cavalry, although forming part of the same legion, and sharing in the movement, protected the Europeans from the Infantry. Among the latter, it was only the Hindustanee portion which revolted, there were some Bheels in the legion who remained faithful. On the preceding day, 21st, about 100 men of the legion had mutinied at Mount Abboo, but as there was a detachment of H. M. 83rd there the mutineers did nothing but hastily escaped. A native Chieftain, the Rae of Sihori, was prompt to render any aid he could to Captain Hall at Mount Abboo. Another portion of the Jodhpore legion was at Jodhpore itself, where the mutiny placed in great peril Captain Monck Mason, British resident at that native State. By his energy he provided an asylum for many ladies and children who had been driven from other stations, but he himself fell by the swords of a body of mutinous troopers, under circumstances of mingled cowardice and brutality.

The state of this part of India during July and August may be summed up in a few words. By the revolt of the Contingents of Scindia, Holkar, and Bhopaul, and of the Jodhpore legion, English residents were driven from station to station in much peril and suffering, and English influence became for a time, almost a nullity; but the native Chieftains for the most, remained faithful, even though their troops revolted; and there were hopes of ultimate success from the arrival of relieving columns belonging to the Bombay Army. Of that army a fragment of regiments occasionally displayed mutinous symptoms but not to such a degree as to leaven the whole mass. What the Officers felt through the treachery of the troops, and what their families suffered during all these strange events, need not be described again, both phases of the revolt have received many illustrations in former pages; but this Chapter may fittingly close with two short extracts from letters relating to the mutinies at the stations of Mhow and Indore. An Artillery Officer commenting on the ingratitude of the

Sepoys towards Commanders who had always used them well, said: I must not forget to mention that Colonel Platt was like a father to the men; and that when he had opportunity of leaving them and joining a European Corps last summer, the men petitioned him to stay. He had been upwards of thirty years with them, and when the mutiny took place he had so much confidence in them that he rode up to their lines before we could get out. When we found him next morning, both cheeks were blown off, his back completely riddled with balls, one through each thigh, his chin smashed into his mouth, and three sabre cuts between the cheek-bone and temple, also a cut across the shoulder and the back of the neck. The following few words are from the letters of a lady who was among those that escaped death by flight from Indore: "I have already given you an account of our three days and three nights of wandering, with little rest and not much food, no clothes to change, burning sun, and deluges of rain, but——and I, perhaps, could bear these things better than others, and suffered less. We found kind friends here and I am in Messrs.—— clothes; every thing we had being gone. The destructive wretches, after we left Indore, commenced doing all the damage they could—cutting up carpets with their tulwars, smashing chandeliers, marble tables, slabs, chairs, &c., they even cut out the cloth and lining of our carriages hacking off the wood-work. The residency is uninhabitable and almost all have lost everything I might have saved a few things in the hour and a half that elapsed between the outbreak and our retreat; but I had so relied on some of our defenders, and felt so secure of holding on, that flight never for a moment occurred to me."—*Chambers' Chronicle of the Indian Revolt.*

But subsequent events show that the rebellious spirit of the contingent troops were too powerful for all that the Scindia could devise to allay it. His Highness was obliged to quit his capital, and the wretched Nana succeeded, happily for a time only, to seat his brother on the *Guddee.* British arms have afterwards regained the kingdom, but the event marks the friendly disposition of the Maharajah, with a force bordering on romance. The following article from the *Friend of India* which is a well-written commentary on the friendship of Scindia, gives a succinct history of the preparations for restoration made by His Highness's faithful subjects and the British Government, pretty well indicating the feeling with which this important event was viewed by them.

"GWALLIOR.—The storm in Central India so long expected has burst at last, and we have for the moment lost a State as powerful as Oude. Serious however as is the occurrence there are considerations which seem to be forgotten, and which if they do not remove at least diminish the danger of the event. The facts, omitted from the bulletins, and not very carefully collated in the papers, are still sufficiently distinct. Sir Hugh Rose who had been instructed to attack Culpee from the Gwallior side found himself compelled to attack from the direction of his march. The main body of the rebels therefore when all hope had ceased fled towards Gwallior, out-marching our troops at the rate of about twenty-five miles a day. Their leader Tantia Topee moved even more rapidly, and appears almost unattended to have arrived in Gwallior by the 26th May. There he drew round him the dicontented, announced the pretensions of the Nana to the Peishwahship and succeeded in organizing a formidable intrigue. How he escaped the vigilance of the Durbar it is not difficult to guess. Scindia's fidelity so often questioned has, it is true, at last been proved by his misfortune. Whatever his desire he certainly did not wish for deposition, or to contest his hereditary sovereignty with a Mahratta *pervenu.* He must however have been deceived, and we should regard with extreme suspicion any stories of compulsion put upon such of his officers as remain.

On the 30th the rebels, about 5,000 strong, were reported in full march upon the capital, and Scindia, sending off an urgent requisition for Europeans, moved at the head of his own forces to the attack. He had with him apparently two regiments of Infantry, twelve hundred Cavalry, his Paigar or personal guard, and some guns. The force was sufficient for victory, but almost in the commencement of the action the intrigues of Tantia Topee became apparent. The left division threw down their arms and fled. The right followed their example, the guns were surrendered, and the battle was left to the Body Guard alone. As in the almost similar circumstances at Indore, the Guard never wavered, they charged three times, and if as reported they left six hundred of their number dead upon the field, their courage was only surpassed by their fidelity. The odds however, were too great. They were outflanked, cut up, and scattered, and the Maharajah was at last compelled to fly. With only 50 followers he fled towards Agra, which he reached on the 3rd instant, escorted by a troop of British horse. The rebels then marched on Gwallior which was surrendered without a stroke, and proceeded to organize a Government on the spot. The Nana was proclaimed Maharajah, and acknowledged at a general parade. The green flag has been unfurled,—an odd ensign for the Hindoo usurper of a Mahratta State—the treasury plundered, Rao

Ram, a disgraced official, appointed premier and the bankers and more respectable inhabitants placed under a reign of terror.

Efforts were also made to strengthen the fort. This place, though naturally strong, being built on the top of an isolated rock, is partially in ruins. The walls are crumbling down while the enormous extent of the works renders their defence at all points almost impossible. It is not moreover like Dowlutabad absolutely impregnable when defended by brave men, the ascent being still practicable for elephants. All round, the plain affords every facility for the operations of Cavalry, and if the rebels venture to stand a siege, escape will be almost impossible. They must die there or evacuate the fort before the arrival of the British now hard upon their heels.

Eight hundred of the 3rd Europeans, 300 of Meade's horse and four guns have been despatched from Agra, while the Culpee force is in full march in the same direction. By the 4th it was at Indoorkee, waiting for the first Brigade which had been detained at Jaloun, and on the junction of the three detachments, the force will comprise nearly three European Regiments, the 14th dragoons, a strong body of Hyderabad and Irregular Cavalry, some European Sappers, a siege train, and three troops of Horse Artillery. Sir Hugh Rose who was lying sick at Cawnpore, has recovered his strength, and his arriva, doubles the strength of the besiegers. Effective resistance to such a force would appear to be almost impossible. The enemy will be shelled out of their fort, and cut to pieces by the cavalry without a hope of retreat.

Even however should they succeed in making good their defences for a time, the evil, serious as it is, is not without compensation. The instinct of the scoundrels now swarming in Bundelcund, Etawah, and the districts nearer Agra, is to converge to any centre which promises a momentary immunity. If the contest last they will swarm out of our territories, leaving us a free base of action, and those means of reorganisation so cruelly required. It is not the concentration but the dispersion of our enemies which is dangerous, and their accumulation in Gwallior where they can be attacked from four sides at once would be a movement rather favourable than embarrassing. It is the more advantageous because in Gwallior we have the allies so greatly missed in our provinces. Scindia, though taken by surprise, is not yet powerless. A strong party are still decidedly in his favour, and his Mahratta Sirdars are said to be arming in his behalf. The villagers in Gwallior bring in supplies with a readiness not exhibited in Oude, and on their assistance depends the accurate and minute information our quartermasters so perpetually fail to collect. The extortions already practised, the excessive cruelty displayed by Tantia Topee throughou Bundelcund, and the constant sense of insecurity must ultimately alienate the population. With their assistance, passive though it may be, the force now advancing ought in the very worst case to reinstate Scindia in two months."—*Friend of India.*

On receiving this gloomy intelligence the public mind in Great Britain was also much affected. England bemoaned the deposition of perhaps her greatest and truest Indian ally with a feeling which was honorable to both. We take the following from the *Times*, which without exaggeration speaks out the national mind with regard to this sad occurrence :—

When the mutinies broke out Scindia and Holkar, whose territories are conterminous and closely adjacent to the disturbed districts, remained faithful to our cause, and the former, who was by far the more powerful of the two, displayed considerable judgment as well as loyalty in the policy he pursued. In virtue of the arrangements subsisting between himself and the British Government, he maintained from the revenues of his principalty a compact and well-disciplined force of more than 5,000 men as a "Contingent" available in aid of the Bengal Army This force now so notorious under the name of the Gwallior Contingent, was organized and officered exactly like our own Sepoy Regiments and proved true to its model in all respects by joining in the mutiny at a very early period. At that time when the safety of British India for the moment trembled in the balance, the proceedings of the Gwallior Contingent were of the utmost consequence, for the march of so strong and well equipped a body upon Delhi, Agra, or Lucknow, might have given a disastrous impulse to the course of affairs. Scindia's measures were taken with great ability. Like other native princes in his position, he retained in his pay, and under his independent control, a certain military force over and above the contingent due to the Bengal establishment and this force he played off against the mutineers. In strength and organization it was decidedly inferior to the contingent, but he augmented it as effectually as the crisis admitted, and as the traitors were vascillating and irresolute, he succeeded for some time in paralyzing their movements, though he never hazarded an engagement with them. In the end the mutinous contingent marched away and took post, as our readers know, at Calpee, but the moment of peril was now past, and the formidable Gwallior force never gave us any trouble, except in the attack made upon General Windham at Cawnpore. The sequel however, of these proceedings, as now announced, is not a little extraordinary.

* * * * * *

It is by no means probable that this fortunate piece of audacity will yield the rebels any material advantage, but the event may well be regarded as bringing definitely under notice the merits of the Prince whose loyalty has now caused his actual expulsion from his capital. We can well afford to recompense with a liberal hand such examples of fidelity. If these mutinies have given us any lesson at all, they have taught us that Native Princes, instead of being our natural enemies in India, are likely to be our best supporters, nor is their support any the less desirable because it may be based on motives of self-interest.

* * * * * *

Holkar, also, like Scindia, though in a less conspicuous degree, has been our steady ally, and the Rajah of Puttiallah rendered us services of such critical importance that it would be hard to exaggerate them. Delhi, the scene of our life and death grapple, stands midway between Puttiallah and Gwallior, and while Scindia was neutralizing the treason of the contingent, the Puttiallah chief, on the other side, was contributing his utmost to the sustenance and reinforcement of Sir Archdale Wilson's army. It is to this Rajah, and to others in the same district, that we are indebted for our supplies during the siege, and for the facilities of communication which enabled the requisite succours to come down from the Punjaub. To remunerate these chieftains with becoming munificence, would be an act not only of justice but of prudence, for they have shown themselves able not only to appreciate British rule, but to support it sagaciously and courageously in times of peril."—*Times*, *21st July*, 1858.

It is gratifying to state that the restoration of the Scindia was as prompt as the political and moral effects staked in it were weighty. The Governor-General's notification announcing the event, is a worthy of record of the achievement :—

"*Fort William, Foreign Department, the 25th June*, 1858.

Notification.—The Hon'ble the President in Council is pleased to direct the republication of the following General order by the Right Hon'ble the Governor-General :—

NO. 1855.

GENERAL ORDER BY THE RIGHT HON'BLE THE GOVERNOR-GENERAL.

Foreign Department, Allahabad, the 24th June, 1858.

The Right Hon'ble the Governor-General has

the highest gratification in announcing that the Town and Fort of Gwallior were conquered by Major-General Sir Hugh Rose, on the 19th instant, after a general action, in which the rebels, who had usurped the authority of Maharajah Scindia, were totally defeated. On the 20th June, the Maharaja Scindia, attended by the Governor-General's Agent for Central India, and Sir Hugh Rose, and escorted by British Troops, was restored to the palace of his ancestors, and was welcomed by his subjects with every mark of loyalty and attachment. It was on the 1st June that the rebels, aided by the treachery of some of Maharajah Scindia's Troops, seized the capital of His Highness' Kingdom, and hoped to establish a new Government under a Pretender in His Highness' Territory. Eighteen days had not elapsed before they were compelled to evacuate the Tow[illegible]and Fort of Gwallior and to relinquish the[illegible]ority which they had endeavoured to P[illegible] The promptitude and success with which [illegible] strength of the British Government has been put forth for the restoration of its faithful ally to the capital of his territory, and the continued presence of British Troops at Gwallior to support His Highness in the re-establishment of his administration, offer to all a convincing proof that the British Government has the will and the power to befriend those who, like Maharajah Scindiah, do not shrink from their obligation or hesitate to avow their loyalty. The Right Hon'ble the Governor-General, in order to mark his appreciation of the Maharajah Scindia's friendship, and his gratification at the re-establishment of His Highness' authority in his ancestral dominions, is pleased to direct that a Royal Salute shall be fired at every principal station in India.

By order of the Right Hon'ble the Governor-General of India.

(Signed) G. F. EDMONSTONE,
Secy. to the Govt. of India,
with the Govr.-Genl.

By order of the Hon'ble the President in Council.

CECIL BEADON.
Offg. Secy. to the Govt. of India."

CHAPTER XXV.

THE following relates about the services rendered by the Nawab of Kurnaul :—

' Mr. LeBas, the Judge of Delhi, after undergoing the greatest peril, escaped from that city to Kurnaul. Soon after his arrival during the interval that preceded the advance of our troops from Umballah *via* Kurnaul, and just as the defection became known when we had no military force near Kurnaul, and all men watched anxiously the conduct of each local chief, the Nawab of Kurnaul came to Mr. Le Bas and addressed him to the following effect :—

"Sir, I have spent a sleepless night in meditating on the state of affairs: I have decided to throw in my lot with yours. My sword, my purse, and my followers at your disposal."

So well did he act up to the engagement thus made, that after the fall of Delhi, a testimonial was put into his hand by Mr. Le Bas, equally honorable to both. As a mark of regard, the Judge gave the Nawab his favorite horse, and a letter of thanks for his public services.

Amongst other marks of devotion to our cause, the Nawab had raised a troop of one hundred horse, arm :d and equipped on the model of the P" auth mounted Police corps. I can speak for usurp. efficiency, as some of these men escorted me, th.er a Native Officer, connected with the Nawab, from Kurnaul to Benares.

I consider the conduct of this Mahomedan Nobleman to deserve special commendation, and I trust that he has received suitable reward. Other Mahomedan Talookdars no doubt professed loyalty, and in some instances, did good service, but few so entirely identified themselves with the cause which in May, 1857, was generally considered by the people the losing one. Many who have recieved great credit for loyalty, were mere watchers of the event—as polite to the mutineers as to us, or as the natives expressed it, keeping their feet in both stirrups. My old friend at Kurnaul was an honorable exception."—*Raiks' Revolt of the North-West Provinces.*

We have already alluded to the services of the Maharajah of Puttiallah, and we quote the following from the *Lahore Chronicle*, giving a very gratifying account of the fidelity of His Highness which was of a more distinguished character than the reader would be prepared to credit :—

"The services of the Chiefs of the Cis-Sutlej States, which were noticed in our columns the other day, deserve at our hands some thing more than passing acknowledgment, and when we have had to record time after time, acts of perfidy and black villainy on the part of too many whom gratitude or interest should have bound to our cause, it is a pleasing task to turn from such scenes to the contemplation of the fidelity and zealous friendship displayed by the Chiefs of the Sikh nation at the present time.

The steady alliance and hearty co-operation of the Maharaja of Puttiallah is not now recorded for the first time. It is a matter of history how faithfully his ancestors have adhered to the treaty drawn up between Sir C. Metcalfe and the reigning chief of the time. This fidelity, though sorely tried, has never been shaken. Lord Dalhousie has recorded in his letters to Sir Charles Napier his opinion of the staunchness of our ally which was shewn in the most unmistakeable manner, and from the commencement of the present rebellion, his acts have been such as we might from his antecedents have confidently expected.

Immediately on the news of the Delhi massacre reaching the Commissioner of Umballa, he at once sent for the Rajah of Puttiallah, with whom he held consultation which resulted in the united forces of Puttiallah and Jheend being pushed forward almost to the gates of Delhi, thus saving the country between Umballa and the rebel city from falling a prey to anarchy and plunder. His soldiers have been called upon to render service in Saharunpore. They have aided in recovering the lost territory of Hissar and Sirssa, whilst throughout the length and breadth of the Cis-Sutlej States properly so called, his horsemen and foot soldiers are to be seen in every direction. Whilst aiding us with men, he has not been backward in supplying the real sinews of war, and we hear that he has placed several lakhs of rupees at the disposal of our Government. We have heard too of his princely liberality to the unfortunate fugitives who were rescued mainly through his exertion, from the murderous clutches of the Hissar villains. He fed and clothed and entirely equipped them and gave a general order throughout his dominions that they were to be treated with utmost respect and kindness.

Such facts as these deserve prominent notice and require some recognition at the hand of the British public who will only require to understand the position he holds with regard to us, fully to appreciate the services rendered. That strenuous endeavours were made to corrupt the fidelity of the Maharajah of Puttiallah, we have good authority for believing, and at the outset he had grave doubts of the fealty of some of his own soldiers. But that he himself never entertained one iota of hostility we have equal good authority for asserting, and the remarkable alacrity which he displayed in our cause, speaks sufficiently for itself and requires no further comment. The importance to the British rule of the fidelity of this Prince cannot be overrated. Had he proved untrue, the whole of the country between the Jumna and Sutlej would have risen *en masse*, and if the European force at Umballah had not been annihilated, it would at best have only been able to fight its way back to the Punjab. And if the Sikhs in the Cis-Sutilej had turned against us, who dare say what the result would have been. Suffice it to point out that the road to Delhi would have been closed to our reinforcements, and if this were all, the evil would then have been considered small to what might be expected. But we rejoice to record the fidelity of our ally and would desire prominently to bring forward such instances as this of friendly co-operation, in the hope that they may receive some suitable acknowledgment.

It is not our desire or province at present to urge on the Government the consideration of the reward which is to be given for faithful service rendered. This may be safely deferred till Delhi is taken, but we trust that the British public and our gracious Queen will not be slow to recognize the aid rendered to Englishmen in the hour of need. There are other things dear to men of high feeling, besides lands and money, and we will venture to affirm that an honorary title and the thanks of the British Parliament could not be more suitably bestowed, or more gratefully appreciated by any than the Maharajahs of Puttiallah and Jheend.

In putting forth prominently the services of the Maharajah of Puttiallah we only do justice to our ally. He is at the head of the Sikh confederacy, is confessedly the most powerful of the Chiefs, and his force now employed in our service cannot number less than 10,000, numerically equal to the contingent furnished by Sardinia in the Crimean war; but infinitely surpassing that force in the moral influence which its presence amongst our rank bring to bear.

But though the Rajah of Jheend has furnished fewer men because his resources are smaller, yet his services are not less important. With a small but well trained band he personally took the field at the commencement of the campaign and has gallantly mixed in the thick of the fight and endured with his men the burning heat and the drenching rain. The record of these facts will be quite sufficient to secure their own reward."—*Lahore Chronicle, August* 12.

For comments on these displays both politically and morally important, we shall avail ourselves of the brilliant pen of the *Times*. That great journal thus speaks of the conduct of the Native Princes after having received intelligence of the forwardness with which they came to the aid of the British Government :—

"The most comprehensive, however, of the inferences suggested by the last despatches relates to the conduct of the Native Princes of India. The general reader may hardly be aware, perhaps, of the extent to which States of this character are still preserved under the supremacy of the British Government. We are usually supposed to have pursued the policy of annexation with some degree of rigour, but, although the dominions under our immediate control have certainly been augmented by escheats and confiscations bringing large territorial acquisitions to the Supreme Government, the number of chiefs still enjoying a qualified independence, and secured in the undisturbed possession of very considerable domains, is quite large enough to prove the general tolerance or confidence of our rule. In the North-Western Provinces alone, and in the districts directly adjacent, the Princes, established in Governments of greater or less importance, with armies of more or less significance at their command, were numerous enough to at once turn the scale against us at the commencement of the insurrection. It must be remembered that when the traitorous Sepoys, after breaking out into overt mutiny at Meerut, raised the standard of military rebellion at Delhi, our force in those parts, disproportioned in itself to the strength of the enemy, was still further weakened by its almost complete isolation. The troops forming the only British army in the field against the insurgents had been drawn from Umballah and Simla, and were joined by the Meerut division as they marched by way of Kurnaul to Delhi. But for these necessary operations there was at that time hardly any sufficient or practicable base. Neither Umballah nor Meerut could answer our demands in this respect; for, though the latter place represented a considerable military station, it offered few resources, and, in fact, the great North-Western arsenal of the Government was Delhi itself—the very city we were besieging. At the moment it was not known that the Punjab would be secured to our cause, and moreover, its authorities and its garrisons were mainly at the remotest extremity of the province, on the Afghan frontier. The Punjab itself, too, is by no means conterminous with our North-Western Provinces, where the rebellion was evidently localized. Between these districts and the Sutty, which forms the eastern frontier of the Punjab; a system of small States was interposed, known in Indian nomenclature as the Cis-Sutlej States, and governed by Native Princes of Sikh extraction. It is obvious that on the loyalty and friendship of these chieftains our communications with the Punjab would depend. To the North, again, were the Hill Rajahs, each with his quota of power, to be exercised for our benefit or disadvantage, while in the more immediate vicinity of Delhi, and throughout Rohilcund and the Doab, a considerable body of Hindoo and Mahomedan Princes disposed of more or fewer resources in their respective domains.

It is not a little interesting to observe the almost uniform fidelity with which these chiefs preserved their allegiance to the British Government. Had it not been, in fact, for their signal and active sympathies we could never have established or maintained our position in the face of the mutineers at Delhi. That we should eventually have reconquered the territory, is true enough, but except for the aid of Native Princes at that critical moment we must, in all probability, have lost Upper India for the time. The communications with Calcutta, it should be recollected, were then interrupted, and, indeed, Calcutta had no succours to despatch. Reinforcements from the Punjab could only arrive after some suspense, and then through the co-operation of these Native States, so that the force before Delhi depended virtually for its resources on the Nawabs and Rajahs of the country. That in some instances these chiefs should turn against us in our adversity was of course to be anticipated; but, as a rule, and in the great majority of cases their behaviour left nothing to be desired. The Rajahs of the Cis-Sutlej States threw themselves at once into our cause, lent us the aid of their retainers for forage and escort duties, kept open our communications with the Punjab, brought provisions in abundance to the camp, and effectually protected our rear. The Rajah of Jheend not only added his handful of troops to ours, but actually marched at the head of his own men. The fidelity and good offices of the Rajah of Putteallah are deservedly eulogized, as our readers will observe this evening, in a communication on the best authority, and intelligence we have ourselves received, enables us to confirm this testimony to his extraordinary services. He has relieved us of an infinity of duties, and discharged them with marvellous success. His country intervenes directly between Delhi and the Punjab, and its resources, very considerable in extent, have been placed unreservedly at our disposal. "In fact," says one of our correspondents, writing from the spot, "whatever we have not got, or don't know how to get, we ask him for, and he must somehow or other supply the deficiency." Even money has been advanced to us largely by these Cis-Sutlej chiefs, though if the truth is to be confessed, our previous dealings with them in such matters were not characterized by very great generosity.

If we extend our view to territories somewhat more removed from the principal scene of action we find the same prevalence of sympathy and the same rarity of disaffection. In Rajpootana the Native Princes are certainly giving no countenance to the insurgents, and, to all appearance, are faithful to the British Government. The Mahratta Princes, Scindia and Holkar, have pronounced for us, and are to be credited, perhaps, with the tranquillity still announced from Central India. In Bundelcund, also, we have received the aid of the native Lords, while from Cashmere our ally the late Gholab Singh, whose policy is maintained by his successor promised us some 30,000 troops and £750,000.* In direct contrast with these features of loyalty and good service we ought to place the general treachery of the "Contingents," or forces raised from the resources of these native chiefs, but organized and officered by ourselves. These troops have in most cases mutinied and joined the insurrection against us, while their immediate masters remain faithful. Wherever, in fact, we created battalions like Sepoy battalions, they behaved in the same manner; wherever the native chief appealed to his own private retainers, they followed him to our side. They might not present specimens of high military excellence, but their services to us as auxiliaries have been invaluable. It was a "Contingent" force which has just given the most recent example of mutiny in the little Mahomedan principality of Bhopaul."—*Times.*

CHAPTER XXVI.

WITH reference to the good feeling and eminent services of the Native Princes and their people, the local journals have maintained a discreditable silence which could

* The subsequent services of the Nepalese are too well known to be alluded to here.—COMPILER.

only be attributed to that morbid jealousy which has been fanned by the so-called antagonism of race. There have however been exceptions which, we are sorry to say, are very few. In the following article on the subject which we quote from the *Bombay Telegraph and Courier*, the reader will find that while the writer cordially records the good offices of the great landholders, also notices with the same readiness but not the less regret the reward which many unfortunates among them have received from the spirit of vengeance which mostly ruled at the time the actions of the officials invested with the power of trying the State offenders.

"When the storm of rebellion burst at Meerut and Delhi last year, and when regiment after regiment threw off their allegiance, men turned with anxiety and trembling to discern, what part the Native Princes of India would take in the terrible struggle about to ensue. Amongst our allies, tributaries, and independent states, we had at the commencement of the revolt :—

	Population.
The Raja of Mysore	3,000,000
The Nizam	10,000,000
The Guickwar	2,000,000
Bhopal	5,000
Kotah	6,500
Boondee	2,500
Travancore	6,000
Cochin	2,000
The Rajpootana Princes viz. :—	
Joudpore, Jeypore, Oodepoore, Bikaneer, Jeysulmeer, and numerous other principalities, Holkar, Kattiawar, Guzerat, and Mahratta Princes and chiefs &c. &c.	15,000,000
Scindia's Dominions	4,000,000
Total.........	34,022,000

Our situation was therefore one of extreme peril The Nizam was doubtful ; we had annexed Oude, and his dominions had been again and again threatened. The Guickwar had been frequently slighted, if not insulted. The Rajpootana princes had many wrongs to redress, and in fact, almost every Rajah and Chief, controlling a population of thirty-four millions and a quarter, had grievances for which they had been in vain seeking redress for the last fifty years. Their petitions had been spurned, their memorials "burked," and their agents, when they presumed to call at Leadenhall Street, snubbed. It was, therefore, but little wonder that with the Moghul empire proclaimed at Delhi, Oude in arms, and 80,000 sepoys in

16

open revolt, we should turn with apprehension and anxiety, to watch the part the Rajahs, we have mentioned, would take in the impending conflict. Had they ranged themselves against us, they would have driven us into the sea; but, strange to say, the leading Kings of Hindoostan remained faithful to the last. Out of the whole population of thirty-four millions and a quarter, we do not think more than fifty thousand joined the ranks of the insurgents, and these were headed by chiefs of small note. The Ranee of Jhansi, Tantia Topee and other petty princes of Central India were incited to rebellion, principally through ignorance and a desire to support the pretensions of Dhundoo Punt, commonly called the Nana Saheb. Their petty disaffection, however, is more than a thousand times counterbalanced by the services rendered by the Puttialla Raja, at the siege of Delhi and of Salar Jung, the Dewan of the Nizam at Hyderabad. Even princes who were in London, when they heard of the crisis, forgot their grievances and hurried out to the scene of danger for the purpose of placing their services at the disposal of the Indian Executive;—amongst the foremost of whom was the Nawab of Surat and the Ameer of Khyrpore. Chiefs came forward with offers of assistance who had been most unjustly subjected to the operation of the East India Company's regulations in their own capitals. As an example we may mention the name of the Thacor of Bhownuggur, who offered to equip and place at the service of Government 500 horse and 500 foot—a contingent which would have been of great service to us now in Guzerat. The offer was, however, declined, and this decision of Government acted as a damper upon others, who were compelled to remain passive spectators instead of actors in the struggle. That there were some chieftains who only waited to see which way the balance went to throw themselves against us cannot be doubted; but after a careful examination we are of opinion that the Princes of India were, upon the whole, favourably disposed towards us, and that if Lord Canning had hoisted the English standard and marched in person through Oude on his way to Delhi, proclaiming that all who were not for us were against us, almost every Raja in the land would have joined him and the rebellion would have been crushed in a day. He, however, lost the golden moment, and the princes of India isolated and without unanimity of action, could do nothing but remain passive. Their own people in many instances rebelled, and some were absolutely drawn into the vortex of revolt against their own inclination. Others again fortified their castles, manned their ramparts and gathered together their retainers; so that in the event of the mutineers paying them a visit and in the absence of British troops, they might be prepared to receive them. But even this measure of necessary and commendable precaution has been the means of placing in great peril some chiefs of unswerving loyalty and undoubted fidelity. Advantage has been taken of these preparations by designing men; and chiefs who never dreamed of treason have been denounced as conspirators against the State. Their very loyalty has been made the pitfall of their ruin, and unless Government exercise great judgment and discernment, the most fatal mistakes may be committed. As it was in Ireland in 1798, so will it be in India in 1858, unless great caution is used. The spy and the informer will tread upon the necks of the nobles of the land, and honest men will fall victims to the machinations of knaves and scoundrels. There are native gentlemen now pining in prison, who have been denounced to Government by personal enemies as being guilty of treason against the State, and who are as innocent of any thing of the kind as Sir Colin Campbell or Sir James Outram. They have been made the victims of foul conspiracies, and although the charges upon which they are arraigned, would not stand for a moment before either a judge or jury, yet they have had to swelter in a crowded prison, during all these hot months, and even now see no immediate prospect of a trial. There is no doubt that the times are emergent, that we have passed through great perils, and that the hands of the Executive should be vested with great powers, but at the same time the subject, let him be prince or peasant, should have stern and impartial justice. We have no wish to offer any adverse criticism upon the measures of Government. In this Presidency the acts of the administration have been admirable in the extreme. We merely wish to put Lord Elphinstone and those around him upon their guard. Evil-minded men are taking advantage of the times to satiate old feuds, and we are sure there is not an Englishman in these parts who would not regret, were even one innocent man to perish or fall a victim to the machinations of the spy and the informer.

* * * * *

Several men of note have lately been tried by a military commission, but this is not we think the best tribunal which might be constituted. Upon men taken red-handed like the King or Delhi and Raja of Shorapoor, military men are the best qualified to sit in judgment ; but where the case is complicated, where perjury has to be dealt with and a multitude of native witnesses examined, men accustomed to analize evidences ought to form the Court. It is in our power now to determine whether we shall rule India for a day or for centuries. A nice discrimination and a noble clemency towards all who are worthy of it, will do more towards consolidating our sovereignty in the East than a million of bayonets. A great distinction should be made between a mutinous soldiery and a rebellious people. While we would visit every village with punishment that refused a shelter to our wandering countrymen, and their helpless wives and children, yet we would spare those inhabited by misguided men against whom no other crime could be urged, save disloyalty and disobedience. The eyes not only of India but of the whole of Asia are upon us, and by the line of conduct which we now pursue, will it be determined whether our rule is to be loved or detested. Justice forbids us to be cruel, and while we are stern we can also be humane. In the immediate vicinity of Lord Canning, Sir John Lawrence or Lord Elphinstone, the sternest justice will be administered—but in remote districts unless the stictest vigilance is exercised—to reward the innocent and punish the guilty, will be a work of very great difficulty.

* * * * *

It is quite beyond the power of man to judge of the intent, and until he is gifted with omniscient powers, he ought to be careful how he deals with others upon mere suspicion. It is at all times difficult to condemn upon circumstantial evidence, and at the present time to do so would be both an injustice and a crime. We would hold all men guiltless, who had not committed some overt act, and against whom the strongest and most incontrovertible proof of treason could not be obtained, such is the course which the enlightened statesmen of England would recommend, and such is the line of conduct which will no doubt be eventually followed in India. Even the most prejudiced are beginning to perceive, that the hour of blind vengeance is passed. A hundred lives have been destroyed for every one that was taken by the murderers at Cawnpore and Delhi; the dark day of retribution is over; the fallen have been avenged; the Eternal is satisfied, and his Rainbow of Mercy is set in the sky!"—*Bombay Telegraph and Courier, May 31st*, 1858.

The following is from the narrative of escape of a Delhi fugitive:—

"You will be surprised to learn that Mr. and Mrs. Hollguette have been miraculously saved in Delhi, together with Mr. A.'s family. Mr. A.'s girl died of cholera. The Roman Catholic Padre and Mr. Pereira, late Printer of the *Delhi Gazette*, are also in existence there. Mr. Hollguette in his note, dated the 20th instant, states that he and his wife with other Christians, 14 in number, were dragged to the Kotwalee, where they were kept in durance for some days, after which some good Samaritan of a Hindoo sheltered them; and they had to beg for their daily food from the Hindoos they are now living with the Padre, but are in very distressed circumstances."—*The Phœnix, November* 18, 1857.

The following is a gratifying picture of Native feeling in Agra on the reception of the intelligence of the Fall of Delhi. The houses of the Native inhabitants were richly illuminated and the rejoicings went as merrily as a marriage bell. We are of opinion, (despite the writer we quote) that these public demonstrations are significant of great facts the moral effects of which will not have failed to be duly judged by those, who ever reflected on the destinies of the empire in those days when Delhi, the stronghold of the Sepoys, remained unwrested, and Hindustan proper was a wide sea of disaffection and treason.

"Yesterday the Agra native community anxious to testify their loyalty towards the English Government, resolved to illuminate the city and indulge in other festivities in honor of the fall of Delhi. Mounting a diminutive Tat I wended my way to the gala scene and soon mingling amongst the sable mob, became one of the most interested and amused of the numerous spectators that had assembled. The mild Hindoo was there in his Sunday vest and evidently enjoyed the scene and no wonder considering several months have elapsed since, they have been permitted to congregate in such large numbers so close to the vicinity of the Fort. Many followers of the Prophet likewise attended, but it was very evident by their sullen demeanour, &c., that the illuminations were none of their getting up. Had the Agra European population suffered the fate of their poor countrymen at Cawnpore we should have had every Mussulman in the city illuminating his house, emulating in fact the zeal of the London trade people and citizens during the great peace rejoicings. The Agra sight-seers conducted themselves in a very orderly manner; no row whatever took place, and no doubt when the country people hear of the *tamasha* they will follow the example of their Agra brethren. Doubtless many of your readers consider these native tokens of loyalty as all humbug, and as far as sincerity is concerned I'm of their opinion; but no matter what are the motives that induce the natives to express their joy at our successes, still the effect upon the low classes is good and all in our favor. A Sikh Gooroo many years resident in this city appeared very anxious that the affair should go off well, he gave a large nautch in the evening, and throughout the whole proceedings a smile of triumph played upon his countenance."—*Delhi Gazette* quoted by the *Phœnix, November* 23, 1857.

Here is a brief record of the success which attended the efforts of a Native Chief in fighting on behalf of British Government with a party of mutineers :—

"The Keraolee Rajah's troops have attacked a party of the Indore mutineers, who attempted to cross the Chumbul into his territory. Some were cut up, some drowned, in trying to swim across the Chumbul, and some were apprehended and are now in custody."—*The Phœnix, Nov.* 25, 1857.

The following is taken from the depositions of Quarter Master Serjeant. Bradshaw, of the late United Malwa Contingent, giving an account of his sufferings on the outbreak at Mehidpoor. He says :—

"After leaving Oujein by great difficulty, arrived at Indore on the 10th, where His Highness the Maharajah showed him (Bradshaw) the greatest kindness and provided him with clothes, shoes, food and plenty of wine and did his best to make him as comfortable as he could,—his behaviour is beyond praise. He arrived at Mhow at half past eleven A. M. on the 11th, accompanied by one Subadar and thirty-five men of all ranks belonging to the Contingent. They behaved most gallantly and admirably well; they are Hindoos, and their conduct in such times is beyond all praise.—*Poona Observer* quoted by the *Phœnix*, *Nov.* 30, 1857.

CHAPTER XXVII.

NARRATIVE OF THE ESCAPE OF MR. BROWN OF THE "DELHI GAZETTE" PRESS.

The narrative is full of the incidents common during those days of fights and dangers. But if it gives a painful account of the sufferings to which Mr. Brown was exposed, it also pointedly marks the good will and friendship of the non-military Natives, especially the Hindus, towards the Europeans, and the gratitude of servants and others towards those who benefited them, which have been so remarkably illustrated in the foregoing pages :—

"On Monday May 11th, 1857, all the Christian Compositors were present at the Pre ni consequence of a message having been received about 6 A. M. from the Electric Telegraph Office, to the effect that the mutineers of Meerut were coming on to Delhi, and might be expected in about two hours, this was printed ; and circulated in the station by the usual office chuprasies. The clerks and natives also had apparently fled to the office for protection. People were in great alarm on account of this news. About 8 or 9 o'clock the mutineers did arrive, but it was not till midday that the Bazaar people and the rabble of the town entered the *Delhi Gazette* Press. We still believed that there was more safety in the "Press" than elsewhere. We could not resist them when they came in, as with the exception of the usual guard of nujeebs, four in number, we had not any arms, and the assailants had a very large party of Goojurs with them, who, as well as themselves, were armed, some of us had, before they got into the places, caused our heads to be shaved and put on portions of native dress that the native Compositors lent us, some of us hid in the Tykhannas (apartments under ground used for their coolness in the hot weather.) The rabble commenced with clubs and iron-bound lattees to break every thing they could lay their hands on, demolishing, as far as they could, the Iron Presses, and breaking every thing they could, each man took as much type of all kinds as he could, they pulled out the chokats of the windows and doors, and after doing as much harm as they could, set fire to the cases, the library, the house, and destroyed every thing, the roof (pucka) of the house subsequently fell in. They did not seem at all inclined to hurt the natives of the establishment, who generally said if they had been armed they would have defended the property. I heard that some of the Christian Compositors were killed. But I and three others escaped by the gate of the Tykhanna into the river, and wandered to the north until we arrived at Sir Theophilus' garden, and hid ourselves in some ruined outhouses belonging to the estate; here we remained for two or three hours, and then returned to the river, close to the office, hiding ourselves as well as we could in it and the sandbank, until night, when we got under the Dhobie's large gumlahs which are used to boil the clothes in. On Tuesday morning we woke early and saw the houses, occupied by the Christians, in flames on every side ; they were blazing in every direction, and as the noise was great, we had no alternative, but to remain, hungry as we were, for we had not had a mouthful to eat since we escaped, under the gumlah ; in the course of the day we saw the native book-keeper and some of the natives on the walls of the city on which the Press is built, we dared not speak to them for fear of attracting notice from the sepoys on the walls elsewhere. Thus passed Tuesday the 12th May, we were very fortunate that the Dhobee did not come to work, we suppose there was none for them. On Wednesday, we would scarcely sustain ourselves, the pangs of hunger were so strong, and to appease them we constantly drank water, it was necessary to do something, so we left the gumlah and getting into the river passed up towards cantonments with the view of swimming to the opposite bank. I had 10 rupees, to my three companions, amongst whom was Mr. Pereira, the printer, I gave a rupee each, and tying up the remaining seven rupees twisted them between my toes ; we accomplished our desire and crossed the river, but no sooner had we landed than we were attacked by a party of Goojurs, they stripped us of our clothes, and threw us each a small piece of cloth. In their fright my companions had dropped their rupees into the river. Again we crossed the river, returned to our gumlahs and thought ourselves fortunate, even starving as we were, to save our lives, but at dusk I mustered courage to get into the Tykhanna and passing into the house and through the compound, went away to my house not very far from the Press. The others did not accompany me. I knocked at my door, this aroused some natives who hailed me and asked, "Who was there," I replied "Gholam Navees," but as soon as they heard my voice, they cried out "Ferringhee uya."—I then ran away into the main-road, and about 40 Mussulmans soon surrounded me, I recognised two men among them who were relations of the Compositors and friends of mine and said "have you been so long my neighbours and would now kill me?" They carried me to the Thanna of the Cashmere gate, and gave me up to the Daroga, he was friendly to me and got rid of the crowd, by telling them that I should be sent to the King who would judge me. He put me into an inward room, and when all was quiet, about half an hour afterwards, he sent two men with me and told them to convey me to some distance so that I might have a chance of escape. I accompanied them for about half a mile, when we met a Hindoo Sepoy coming towards us, these two men pointed out that I was a Ferringee and the Sepoy brought up his musket to my chest and was searching for a percussion cap in his *cummerbund* when I cried out in Bengallee and said I was a petty merchant from Calcutta lately arrived in Delhi. I gave an oath on the cow and on Kallee and was not harmed, they had left me and the Mussulmans said that as the Sepoy had not killed me they would not. I then went on towards the Magazine and met with one of the Mussulman apprentices of the Press, and as I was almost dead with hunger, and having all this time supported myself with water—I cried bitterly to him and asked him to save me for the night; he took me to a mosque and told the Cazee that the King had ordered me to be converted to Islamism at once and that no one was to harm me. The Cazee bathed me and made me repeat the Kulma and the apprentice brought me bread and wine, a pajama and koortee. Not the least attempt was made to circumcise me; had that been the case, I could not have resisted for my weakness. I was named Shaik Abdoola. The apprentice slept by me in the mosque, and early in the morning he returned home to prepare breakfast for himself, promising to send me some. In the meantime lots of people came into the mosque, asking " where is this Christian who has been converted?" Others said " kill him, he has only become Mahomedan to save his life." The Cazee replied, " To kill him will be no gain to us, he is now of us," others said " still it is better to kill him for if the Ferringees come, he will betray us." I managed to pass out of the mosque in the crowd as soon as I could, and in the street met our jemadar pressman, we recognised each other, and he, though a Mussulman, did not betray me, but advised me to go off to Calcutta, for said he " I can not protect you and intend getting to Calcutta as soon as I can." He was a native of Calcutta. Again I returned to the gumlahs and found my companions, still there walking about, this was on Thursday morning and we agreed to separate some distance from one another, so as not to be so distinctly seen, and got at last over the bridge of boats on to the Meerut road. I arrived first at some walled place the name of which I do not know, and waited a long time for my companions, but they did not arrive, I thought they had been arrested, perhaps murdered, so I went on towards Gazeedeenuggur. I was again stripped of every thing I had by the Goojurs and arrived at Gazeedeenuggur at six in the evening stark naked. I went to the Jemadar and represented myself as a Mussulman who had been plundered of every pice I had, besides my clothes; he gave me bread and dholl and allowed me to sleep there. The next morning I went on to Boolundshuhur where I met James Bambert Jones, an Eurasian, and the head Clerk of the Magistrate's office, he had some relations at Delhi, who had been massacred, he asked me many questions to convince himself that my story was true; when he found it to be so, he gave me to eat and went to the Magistrate to tell him; the Magistrate, he said, did not believe my story, but the Clerk still protected me and giving me two annas pice and a piece of cloth, set me on my road, he did not give me more for fear of my attracting notice and of being robbed. I begged my way to Agra, as the people would not admit me in the serais,—they would not admit any strangers. On the 8th day or thereabouts I got to Agra, and was almost immediately employed by Mr. Longden, the Superintendent of the Orphan Press. (He did not go to the *Delhi Gazette Branch*, being a Calcutta man and quite unacquainted with its position for the people belonging to it, but he knew some of the "hands" at Secundra.) When Mr. Longden went into the Fort, the Compositors, &c., remained there armed to protect the Establishment at Secundra, so we did not go, we were a great many and thought ourselves quite secure. When the battle took place, and the Establishment was destroyed, I got refuge in an old mosque and my servant fed me for three days, after which I left Secundra, disguised as a Mahomedan, I feared to go to the Fort as a Christian for fear of the Mussulmans, nor into the Fort in a Mahomedan dress, lest the European sentries should shoot me!

I got out of Agra on the 11th July and reached Cawnpore in safety, still in a native dress; on the 18th a soldier of the 64th Queen's, when marching to Bithoor, captured me, believing me to be a sepoy, and took me to an officer, with whom I spoke and read English, he was soon convinced that I was a Christian and advised me to report myself to General Havelock. I did so in the evening when we arrived at Nuwabgunge, and after enquiring about the roads for, he dismissed, giving me two rupees and telling me to remain in Camp. I went and lived with the European soldiers who were very kind to me. I accompanied the Camp in the battle of Mungulwarra, Oonow and Bussoorgunge, and afterwards returned to Cawnpore and Bithoor. Subsequently I came on to Allahabad with the sick and wounded, under the charge of Apothecary Price, and subsequently to Benares where I am employed by the Lieutenant-Governor and where I found out my old employer yourself."—*Friend of India quoted by the Phœnix, December* 5, 1857.

CHAPTER XXVIII.

ESCAPE OF MR. JAMES CAVANAUGH.

THE "escape" of Mr. Cavanaugh has a tinge of romance befitting the days of knight-errantry which Walter Scott has immortalized in his memorable pages. The public, with a deserving generosity, has awarded the full meed of its approbation on this unrivalled piece of personal heroism, and the Government, with a worthy liberality, has rewarded Mr. Cavanaugh's gallant and conspicuous services. But there was a rival in the field—a collaborateur in the race,—one who underwent with the Christian hero the same sufferings and bore with the same glorious patience the stupendous difficulties which surrounded their perilous journey, and who displayed a greater moral courage inasmuch as he acted against his instinct and allied himself with a representative of foreign blood and a follower of an "infidel" creed,—and unto this man we ask his dues fully and without stint to be rendered. Kunonjolal and Cavanaugh are twins in this respect, and they deserve equal rewards and equal treatment. An iota less of this to one will be held tantamount to an insult to the other. We believe Kunonjolal has been rewarded for his services but we have reasons to think not *fully* and adequately. There can be no doubt that without Kunonjolal, without his unflinching courage, his fertility of resources to protect his co-partner, his unshaken fidelity, and his strong intelligence, the heroism of Cavanaugh would have remained a dream in the author's mind. Inasmuch therefore as the public and Government value Cavanaugh's services they should consider and weigh Kunonjolal's contribution to them. We trust the heathen hero will be distinguished by a Government which looks with an equal eye upon the merits and services of a black man and white in the same degree as has the Christian hero been :—

"Narrative of my escape from the British entrenchment at Lucknow to the Camp of Sir Colin Campbell, near Bunnee, for the purpose of acting as his guide in his advance for the relief of the besieged garrison.

While passing through the entrenchment of Lucknow about 10 o'clock A. M., on the 9th instant, I learnt that a spy had come in from Cawnpore, and that he was going back in the night as far as Alum Bagh, with despatches to his Excellency Sir Colin Campbell, the Commander-in-Chief, who, it was said, was approaching Lucknow with five or six thousand men. I sought out the spy, whose name is * * * * * * and who was in the Court of the Deputy Commissioner of Dariabad before the outbreak in Oude. He had taken letters from the entrenchment before, but I had never seen him till now. I found him intelligent, and imparted to him my desire to venture in disguise to Alum Bagh in his company. He hesitated a great deal at acting as my guide, but made no attempt to exaggerate the dangers of the road. He merely urged that there was more chance of detection by our going together, and proposed that we should take different roads and meet outside of the city to which I objected. I left him to transact some business, my mind dwelling all the time on the means of accomplishing my object.

I had some days previously witnessed the preparation of plans, which were being made by direction of Sir James Outram, to assist the Commander-in-Chief in his march into Lucknow for the relief of the besieged, and it then occurred to me that some one, with the requisite local knowledge, ought to attempt to reach His Excellency's camp beyond or at Alum Bagh. The news of Sir Colin Campbell's advance revived the ideas and I made up my mind to go myself at 2 o'clock after finishing the business I was engaged upon. I mentioned to Colonel R. Napier, Chief of Sir James Outram's staff, that I was willing to proceed through the enemy to Alum Bagh if the General thought my doing so would be of service to the Commander-in-Chief. He was surprised at the offer, and seemed to regard the enterprise as fraught with too much danger to be assented to, but he did me the favor of communicating the offer to Sir James Outram, because he considered that my zeal deserved to be brought to his notice.

Sir James did not encourage me to undertake the journey, declaring that he thought it so dangerous that he would not himself have asked any officer to attempt it. I however spoke so confidently of success, and treated the dangers so lightly that he at last yielded—and did me the honor of adding that if I succeeded in reaching the Commander-in-Chief my knowledge would be a great help to him.

I secretly arranged for a disguise so that my departure might not be known to my wife, as she was not well enough to bear the prospect of an eternal separation. When I left home about 7 o'clock in the evening, she thought I was gone on duty for the night to the mines, for I was working as an Assistant Field Engineer by order of Sir James Outram.

By 7½ o'clock my disguise was completed, and when I entered the room of Colonel Napier, no one in it recognised me. I was dressed as a Budmash or as an Irregular soldier of the city, with sword and shield, native-made shoes, tight trowsers, and yellow silk koortah over a tight fitting white muslin skirt, a yellow colored chintz sheet thrown round my shoulders, a cream colored turban, and a white waistband or a *kumurbund*. My face down to the shoulders, and my hands to the wrists were colored with lamp-black, the cork used being dipped in oil to cause the color to adhere a little. I could get nothing better, I had little confidence in the disguise of my features, and I trusted more to the darkness of the night; but Sir James Outram and his staff seemed satisfied, and after being provided with a small double-barrelled pistol, and a pair of broad *pyjamahs* over the tight drawers, I proceeded with Kunonjolal to the right bank of the river Goompty, running north of our entrenchment, accompanied by Captain Hardinge of the Irregular Cavalry.

Here we undressed and quietly forded the river, which was only about 4½ feet deep and about a hundred yards wide at this point. My courage failed me while in the water and if my guide had been within reach, I should perhaps have pulled him back and abandoned the enterprise. But he waded quickly through the stream, and reaching the opposite bank, went crouching up a ditch for three hundred yards to a grove of low trees on the edge of a pond where we stopped to dress. While we were here a man came down to the pond to wash, and went away again without observing us.

My confidence now returned to me, and with my Tulwar resting on my shoulder, we advanced into the huts in front where I accosted a matchlockman, who answered to my remark, that the night was cold, " It is very cold, in fact, it is a cold night." I passed him, adding that it would be colder by and bye.

After going six or seven hundred yards further we reached the Iron Bridge over the Goompty, where we were stopped and called over by a native officer, who was seated in an upper-storied house and seemed to me in command of a cavalry picquet whose horses were near the place saddled. My guide advanced to the light and I stayed a little back in the shade. After being told that we had come from Mundeon, (our old cantonment and then in the possession of the enemy,) and that we were going into the city to our homes he let us proceed. We continued on along the left bank of the river to the Stone Bridge, which is about eight or nine hundred yards from the Iron Bridge, passing unnoticed through a number of sepoys and matchlockmen, some of whom were escorting persons of rank in palankees preceded by torches.

Re-crossing the Goompty by this Stone Bridge we went by a sentry unobserved who was closely questioning a dirtily dressed native, and into the chauk, or principal street of Lucknow, which was not illuminated as much as it used to be previous to the siege, nor was it so crowded. I jostled against several armed men in the street without being spoken to, and only met one guard of seven sepoys who were amusing themselves with some women of pleasure.

When issuing from the city into the country, we were challenged by a Choukeedar or watchman, who, without stopping us, merely asked who we were. The part of the city traversed that night by me, seemed to have been deserted by at least a third of its inhabitants.

I was in great spirits when we reached the green fields, into which I had not been for five months. Every thing around us smelt sweet, and a carrot I took from the road side, was the most delicious I had ever tasted. I gave vent to my feelings in a conversation with Kunonjolal, who joined in my admiration of the province of Oudh, and lamentation that it was now in the hands of wretches whose misgovernment and rapacity was ruining it.

A further walk of a few miles was accomplished in high spirits, but there was trouble before us. We had taken the wrong road and were now quite out of our way in the Dilkooshah Park, which was occupied by the enemy. I went within twenty yards of two guns to see what strength they were, and returned to the guide, who was in great alarm and begged I would not distrust him because of the mistake, as it was caused by his anxiety to take me away from the picquets of the enemy. I bade him not to be frightened of me for I was not annoyed, as such accidents were not unfrequent even when there was no danger to be avoided. It was now about midnight. We endeavoured to persuade a cultivator who was watching his crop to show us the way for a short distance, but he urged old age and lameness, and another whom I peremptorily told to come with us, ran off screaming and alarmed the whole village. We next walked quickly away into the Canal, running under the Char Bagh in which I fell several times owing to my shoes being wet and slippery and my feet sore. The shoes were hard and tight and had rubbed the skin off my toes and cut into the flesh about the heels. In two hours more we were again on the right direction, two women in a village we passed having kindly helped us to find it, about 2 o'clock we reached an advanced picquet of sepoys who told us the way after asking where we had come from and whither we were going. I thought it safer to go up to the picquet than to try to pass them unobserved.

Kunonjolal now begged I would not press him to take me into Alum Bagh as he did not know the way in, and the enemy were strongly posted around the place. I was tired and in pain from the shoes, and would therefore have preferred going into Alum Bagh, but as the guide feared attempting it, I desired him to go on to the camp of the Commander-in-Chief which he said was near Bunnee (a village 18 miles from Lucknow) upon the Cawnpore road. The moon had risen by this time, and we could see well ahead.

By 3 o'clock we arrived at a grove of mangoe trees, situated on a plain in which a man was singing at the top of his voice. I thought he was a villager, but he got alarmed on hearing us approach and astonished us too by calling out a guard of twenty-five Sepoys, all of whom asked questions. Kunonjolal here lost heart for the first time, and threw away the letter entrusted to him for Sir Colin Campbell. I kept mine safe in my turban. We satisfied the guard that we were poor men, travelling to Umroula, a village two miles this side of the Chief's Camp to inform a friend of the death of his brother by a shot from the British entrenchment at Lucknow, and they told us the road.

They appeared to be greatly relieved on discovering that it was not their terrible foe, who was only a few miles in advance of them. We went in the direction indicated by them and after walking for half an hour we got into a jheel or swamp, which are numerous and large in Oudh, we had to wade through it for two hours up to our waists in water, and through weeds, for before we found out that we were in a jheel, we had gone too far to recede. I was nearly exhausted on getting out of the water having made great exertions to force our way through the weeds and to prevent the color being washed off my face. It was nearly gone from my hands.

I now rested for fifteen minutes, despite of the remonstrances of the guide, and went forward passing between two picquets of the enemy who had no sentries thrown out. It was near four o'clock in the morning, when I stopped at the corner of a tope or grove of trees to sleep for an hour, which Kunonjolal entreated I would not do, but I thought he overrated the danger, and lying down I told him to see if there was any one in the grove who would tell him where we then were.

We had not gone far when I heard the English challenge " who comes there " with a native accent. We had reached a British Cavalry outpost; my eyes filled with joyful tears and I shook the Seikh officer in charge of the picquet heartily by the hand. The old soldier was as pleased as myself, when he heard whence I had come, and he was good enough to send two of his men to conduct me to the Camp of the advance guard. An officer of Her Majesty's 9th Lancers who was visiting his picquets, met me on the way, and took me to his tent where I got dry stockings, and trousers, and what I much needed, a glass of brandy, a liquor I had not tasted for two months.

I thanked God for having safely conducted me through this dangerous enterprize, and Kunonjolal for the courage and intelligence with which he had conducted himself during this trying night. When we were questioned he let me speak as little as possible. He always had a ready answer, and I feel that I am indebted to him in a great measure more than to myself for my escape. It will give me great satisfaction to hear that he has been suitably rewarded.

In undertaking this enterprize I was actuated by a sense of duty, believing that I could be of use to His Excellency the Commander-in-Chief when approaching for its relief, the besieged garrison which had heroically resisted the attack of thirty times its own number for nearly five months, with its weak and irregular entrenchment; and secondly because I was anxious to perform some service which would ensure to me the honor of wearing our Most Gracious Majesty's Cross.

My reception by Sir Colin Campbell and his Staff was cordial and kind to the utmost degree, and if I never have more than the remembrance of their condescension and of the heart-felt congratulations of Sir James Outram and of all the officers of his garrison on my safe return to them I shall not repine, though to be sure having the Victoria Cross would make me a prouder and happier man.

JAMES CAVANAUGH

Camp Allum Bagh,
24th November, 1857.

The Phœnix, December 18, 1857.

CHAPTER XXIX.

A letter from Nynee Tal, dated the 26th of October, gives us the following :—

"The Nawab of Rampore has behaved very well indeed during these troublous times, he is the only man that has given us any assistance from the plains. The Gurhwal Rajah, like all Paharies, has aided us to his very utmost. When we were last threatened by the 5,000 rebels, from Bareilly, all the Paharies as far as Palee flocked in. Thousands volunteered and came without pay, and actually brought their own grub, and went wherever they were ordered without a grumble. All the headmen of Gurhwal and Kalee Kumaan offered to come to our aid.

These assurances of loyalty have not been few during the mutinies. That there existed an imperative need for them few will now deny, though the crisis has passed. When the general character of the rebellion first came to notice, the public mind in Calcutta and in the neighbourhood was seized with such a fever of panic that the most self-possessed Europeans, evincing a great confidence in Natives, suspected the latter every hour of treacherous intentions. The excitement was so violent that during the night many used to leave their homes and sleep with their family and friends on board the ships and sloops. The leaders of Native Society therefore wisely resolved to record publicly their feelings and views of the conduct of the mutinous soldiery, and to acquaint Government with the same. The first meeting for this purpose was held in the hall of the Hindu Metropolitan College, which was attended by the highest members of the Native Community. The British Indian Association, on the part of the Natives generally, published resolutions expressive of their abhorrence of the conduct and acts of the mutineers, and also of their allegiance to Government Then followed a train of loyal assurances more or less fervid and all directed to the promotion of the noble object of removing every impression that the revolt was sympathized with by the Natives of Bengal. All the addresses with the replies of Government thereto, have been published in the Blue Books on the Mutinies, some of which we have selected for these pages.

Those addresses have an historical importance. They were the signs of the times and the manifestations of the feelings which predominated among the Native Community at the time in regard to the British Government. Through them the future historian will perceive the then temper of the Native mind, both Hindu and Mahomedan. Clamours are still rife that those assurances were hollow and had no intrinsic merit, but we may be allowed to say that they are mere "clamours." Our readers will remember with what rancour and insolence was the conduct of Government impeached for drawing a line of distinction between the rebels and the vast body of the people, and for following a discriminating policy. The reigning Ministry with an advanced intelligence justly dreaded the consequences of a popular outbreak and the advisers of Lord Canning possessing a sufficient knowledge of the Native character recommended a policy which would not irritate the bulk of the population. The Calcutta Europeans could uot however see the justice of this policy, and they accused Government of weakness, want of judgment and courage, and of distrust of English character and resources. The time was thus ripe for an active demonstration on the part of the Natives of the feelings which worked in them, and they did not mistake it. Their loyal addresses defined the character of the revolt and gave effect to the policy of the Government. Then it was that the military aspect of the outbreak became distinct, and the relative position of the State and the people became settled. There have been European residents here, as we have said above, who question the motives of such movements. But the acts and services recorded in these pages, will remain standing proofs of the integrity of the intentions of the movers of these projects. That they fulfilled some purpose may be perceived by calling to mind that translations of these addresses in Hindee, Urdu and Bengalee were extensively circulated among the population to re-assure confidence where it was weakened, to dissipate errors where it might gain ground, and to defeat the machinations of the evil disposed, where they could take effect. The historian, we believe, will not miss the real character of these proceedings of our countrymen, and we are morally certain that they will be valued by posterity as the true picture of the popular mind during the crisis.

TO THE SECRETARY TO THE GOVERNMENT OF INDIA.

Calcutta, May 15th, 1857.

SIR,

As Chairman of a Public Meeting of the Native community convened this day, pursuant to a requisition published in the Daily Journals, I have the honor to forward to you a copy of the Resolutions passed on the occasion, for the information of the Governor-General in Council.

I have, &c.,

RADHACANT, RAJAH BAHADUR,

Chairman.

RESOLUTIONS.

---

1. That the Meeting has, with deep concern and sorrow, learnt of the disaffection manifested by a portion of the native army, and of the atrocities committed by them in some parts of the country, and that it views their mutinous conduct with extreme disgust and horror.

2. That this Meeting contemplates, with the highest and most sincere satisfaction, that the sepoy disaffection has met with no sympathy or encouragement from the civil population of any part of this vast empire, nor has it been shared in by the major portion of the native soldiery; but that the same feelings of loyalty and attachment to the British rule, which they have hitherto been inspired with, still continue to animate them with unabated fidelity.

3. That this Meeting contemplates, with the deepest concern, the lamentable delusion which some of the sepoy regiments appear to be labouring under, and that it desires to record its firm and sincere conviction that the malicious reports which have given rise to such a delusion are not founded upon truth.

4. That this Meeting is of opinion that, should occasion require, it would be the duty of the native portion of Her Majesty's subjects to

render the Government every aid in their power, for the preservation of civil order and tranquillity.

5. That, with a view to give an extensive circulation to the proceedings of this Meeting, it be resolved that translations of the same into the vernacular dialects of the country, be printed and distributed amongst the native population.

6. Resolved that a copy of the Resolutions adopted at this Meeting be forwarded, under the signature of its Chairman, to the Governor-General in Council.

Appendix (A) to further Papers (No. 5, relative to the Mutinies.)

THE SECRETARY TO THE GOVERNMENT OF INDIA TO RAJAH RADHACANT BAHADOOR.

Fort William, May 26th, 1857.

SIR,

I have the honor, by direction of the Governor-General in Council to acknowledge the receipt of the letter which, as Chairman of a Public Meeting of the native community, you yesterday addressed me, forwarding a copy of the Resolutions passed at the meeting.

2. These Resolutions his Lordship has perused

with unmixed satisfaction, and he highly appreciates the loyalty and good sense of the native community of Calcutta, which have led them, at the present juncture to assemble together for the purpose of expressing their abhorrence of the mutinous conduct of some of the native regiments of the Bengal Army; their confidence in the fidelity and attachment of the Native Army in general, and of the people of India, to the British Government; their utter disbelief in the falsely alleged intention of the Government to tamper with the religion of its Hindoo and Mussulman subjects; and their sense of the obligation imposed on the native public to support the Government in the preservation of order and tranquillity.

3. For this manly declaration of their sentiments, the Governor-General in Council returns his sincere thanks to the native community, and he reiterates the assurance so often given, and so steadfastly fulfilled, that the policy of the British Government in India has been, and ever will be, to preserve a position of strict neutrality in matters of faith, to respect all scruples of caste, and to leave its subjects of every creed and class to the free and uninterrupted enjoyment of their religious opinions and observances.

4. The most decisive steps have been taken for the suppression of the revolt, and for the due punishment of guilty men, who have swerved

from their allegiance, and disgraced human nature by acts of the most brutal cruelty.

The Governor-General in Council entirely approves of the intention to print the Resolutions in the vernacular dialects of the country, and circulate them among the native population.

I have, &c.,

CECIL BEADON.

CHAPTER XXX.

FROM THE HONORARY SECRETARY OF THE BRITISH INDIAN ASSOCIATION TO THE SECRETARY TO THE GOVERNMENT OF INDIA.

May 23, 1857.

SIR,—I have the honor to request the favor of your laying the accompanying address of the Committee of the British Indian Association before His Lordship the Governor-General of India.

I have, &c.,

ISSURCHUNDER SINGH,

Honorary Secretary.

TO THE GOVERNOR-GENERAL OF INDIA.

MY LORD,—We, the Presidents, Vice-Presidents, and Committee of the British Indian Association, beg leave to approach your Lordship with the accompanying copy of resolutions which we felt it our duty to record, on hearing of the deplorable events which have lately occurred at Meerut and Delhi. We have also resolved to circulate these resolutions among our countrymen in the interior, and to make known their purport generally by means of their translations. Were we permitted to add any thing to these resolutions it would be an expression of our admiration for, and confidence in, your Lordship's conduct of affairs at this crisis.

We have, &c.,

RADHACAUNT RAJAH BAHADOOR,

RAJAH KALLY KRISHNA BAHADOOR, V. P.

PERTAB CHUNDER SING, *and others.*

Extract from the Proceedings of a Meeting held of the Committee of the British Indian Association, held May 22, 1857.

The Committee of the British Indian Association have heard of the disastrous events which have lately occurred at Meerut and Delhi with deep concern and sorrow.

The Committee view with disgust and horror the disgraceful and mutinous conduct of the native soldiery at those station, and the excesses committed by them, and confidently trust to find that they have met with no sympathy, countenance, or support from the bulk of the civil population of that part of the country, or from any reputable or influential classes among them.

The Committee of the Association record, without hesitation, their conviction of the utter groundlessness of the reports that have led a hitherto faithful body of the soldiers of the State to the commission of the gravest crimes of which military men or civil subjects can be guilty, and the Committee deem it incumbent on them, on the present occasion, to express their deep abhorrence of the practices and purposes of those who have spread these false and mischievous reports.

The Committee earnestly hope for the restoration of peace and good order, which they doubt not will be soon re-established by the vigorous measures which the government have adopted in this exigency.

The Committee trust and believe that the loyalty of their fellow-subjects in India to the Government under which they live, and their confidence in its power and good intentions are unimpaired by the lamentable events which have occurred in the detestable efforts which have been made to alienate the minds of the sepoys and the people of the country from their duty and allegiance to the beneficent rule under which they are placed.

(Appendix (A) to further Papers, (No. 5) relative to the Mutinies.)

THE SECRETARY TO THE GOVERNMENT OF INDIA TO RAJAH RADHACAUNT AND OTHERS.

Fort William, May 25th, 1857.

GENTLEMEN,

1. Your Address and the Resolutions passed by the Committee on the 22nd instant, which were communicated to me in your Honorary Secretary's letter of the 23rd, having been laid before the Governor-General in Council, I am directed to inform you, that his Lordship in Council has received this expression of the sentiments of an influential and intelligent body of Hindoo gentlemen, as to the recent conduct of some of the native regiments, and the motives of those who instigated it, with the highest gratification.

2. The Governor-General in Council is well assured that the rash and criminal acts of which these misguided men have been guilty meet with no sympathy or countenance from the people at large, and that they are viewed with special abhorrence by those who can appreciate the character of the British Government, and who rightly understand the principles by which that Government is guided in the use of its vast power and resources; a signal proof of this has been afforded by the Maharajah Scindia and other chiefs, who, unsolicited, have given prompt and powerful support to the Government, and by the zemindars of the disturbed districts, who have protected British officers from violence, and exerted themselves loyally to check disorders.

3. For a hundred years under British rule, every one has been left at full liberty to worship God according to the dictates of his own conscience, and to do such things as his religion enjoins, and to abstain from those which it forbids. The experience of a century has been lost upon those who can now believe the gross and wicked falsehood that the Government intends or desires to pursue a contrary course; a course by which it could gain no advantage, and which could not fail to excite the indignation and hatred of its subjects.

4. The Committee of the British Indian Association have declared their attachment to

the British Government, and their confidence in its power and good intentions; and they propose, that the Resolutions they have passed, shall be circulated among their fellow-countrymen in the interior. His Lordship in Council has no doubt that these proceedings are well calculated to restore confidence where it has been shaken, and to lead to the best results.

5. The forces at command of the Government are enough to put down all opposition. They have now been brought to bear on the men of the mutinous regiments who are assembled at Delhi; and the Governor-General in Council confidently expects, that, in a few days, the mutiny will be entirely suppressed, tranquillity again established, and condign punishment inflicted upon those who have disturbed the public peace, and aggravated rebellion, by crimes of the most horrible atrocity.

I have, &c.,

CECIL BEADON.

CHAPTER XXXI.

MEMORIAL.

To

F. R. COCKERELL, Esq.,
Magistrate of Hooghly.

Sir,

We, the undersigned Zemindars, Talookdars, and inhabitants of Ooterpara, Bhudderkally, Koterung, Konenuggur, and other adjacent villages, have heard with deep sorrow the melancholy effects of the Sepoy Mutiny. We have to thank Government for the strong and adequate measures adopted to put down that mutiny. The disarming of the sepoys of the Presidency division has tended greatly to allay the fears of the populace. But though disarmed, still they continue disaffected, and the fear of being visited by the deserved punishment of their crimes has made numbers of them desert their posts. These, as well as the men of the 19th and 34th Regiments of Native Infantry, will not, for manifest reasons, go to their homes at present; and private individuals will not entrust their lives and property to men who have proved unfaithful to the best masters they could have served, and have been audacious enough to rise against the authority of Government; the consequence will be that, out of necessity they would be obliged to commit plunder and robbery, and other crimes, to support themselves. With the utmost respect to yourself, as the head of the local police, we beg to observe that the police of the whole district, could it be collected together in one place, would be useless to cope with even a straggling party of fifty disbanded sepoys; but it is well known that this force is scattered over an area of 800 square miles. The vicinity of Barrackpore and Calcutta, and the total inadequacy of the police force in thannah Bydabatty, where there are a single Darogah and a few miserable burkundauzes to guard about 100 square miles of country, can not but increase the alarm of the inhabitants of this part of the district. Even the thannah police, incapable as it is, is ten miles distant from this place and we have neither a military nor municipal force to apply to in case of a sudden attack, of which the probability is increasing every day, from the daily increasing number of disarmed and disbanded sepoys roaming in the country, uncontrolled and in despair, joined with those who had come down from the Upper Provinces, as their relations and comrades of regimental vacancies. To these attacks we can only oppose the nugdees and durwans in the employment of the zemindars and other wealthy men; unfortunately, however, most of these are either relations or intimate acquaintances of the Barrackpore sepoys, who would not, we are certain, hesitate to fraternize on a dangerous crisis. It is not good policy to discharge these nugdees at present, nor can we, in the present disturbed state of the country, collect a large pyke force to cope, not only with the sepoys, but with our own nugdees also; on whose good conduct we had hitherto relied for safety, but which the recent circumstances have proved to be confidence reposed upon undeserving and treacherous men. We would, therefore, pray that you will be good enough to bring these circumstances to the notice of Government, that prompt measures which may appear proper and adequate in the wisdom of Government, may be taken for the safety of our lives and properties from the present imminent danger which threatens us.

But if we are permitted to suggest, we would propose that for immediate safety, a company of European Infantry be stationed at Serampore, from which patrolling parties of twenty-five men each, may be sent to southward and northward to watch over the conduct of the disbanded and deserted sepoys, who have crossed over to this side of she river, and to prevent further crossings.

2ndly. That a local militia or police battalion of 500 men may be raised in this district as well as in Burdwan, composed of Agoories, Gowalas, Bagdees, and Domes, &c., under the control of an European officer, and a few drill serjeants, together with two educated native officers, taken from respectable ranks. Those among us who own zemindaries, hereby tender our services in procuring serviceable men for the purpose of being enlisted, but the mere procuring of men will do little good unless those men receive a sort of military organization, and be kept under proper discipline. We are quite confident that by the prompt and decisive measures pursued by Government, the Sepoy Mutiny will be very shortly put down in the Upper Provinces; yet it must be recollected, that with the mere putting down of the mutiny, a major portion of the sepoy army will be annihilated, a circumstance which will embolden all the budmashes and bad characters of the country, who have been hitherto kept down by the fear of the native troops stationed in different districts; these being joined by the disbanded men and others who will come down from the Upper Provinces in the hope of plunder, will entail upon Government, at least for some years, the necessity of maintaining a local militia or police battalion in several parts of the country. The course recommended will, it is hoped, as an experiment, be found to be of considerable service hereafter.

We have, &c.,

JOYKISSEN MOOKERJEE,

June 17th, 1857. *And Forty-Seven Others*

(Appendix (A) to further Papers, (No. 5) relative to the Mutinies.)

THE SECRETARY TO THE GOVERNMENT OF BENGAL TO THE MAGISTRATE OF HOOGHLY.

Fort William, June 22nd, 1857.

SIR,

I am directed to acknowledge the receipt of your letter of the 20th instant, giving cover to a memorial from certain inhabitants of Ooterpara and other adjacent villages, wherein they express much apprehension, in consequence of the desertions from the ranks of the disarmed Sepoys at Barrackpore, and recommending the entertainment of an additional Police force, consisting of 600 men, of the Agooree and Gowala classes, for the maintenance of order in your district in the event of any disturbance arising.

2. In reply, I am desired to observe that, under Act 17 of 1857, you are employed to arrest the deserters, the number of whom, however, appears to be greatly exaggerated by public apprehension.

3. Under the circumstances represented by you, the Lieutenant-Governor authorizes, as an experimental measure, the organization of a central Police force at the Sudder Station of Hooghly, consisting of people of the classes described in your letter; and should the experiment prove successful, His Honor will be prepared

to authorize its extension to other parts of the district.

I have, &c.,

A. R. Young.

(*Appendix (A) to further Papers (No. 5) relative to the Mutinies*)

Meetings and addresses of this description were also held in, and presented from other parts of the country. Resolutions were passed to the same effect and documents of the same character were addressed to the Governor-General in Council or to the provincial representatives of Government as circumstances required. The following is a list of the parties who made these loyal demonstrations :—

Inhabitants of Bally Dewangunge.
" of Bancoorah.
" of Noakhally.
" of Sylhet.

Zemindars and other inhabitants in the Zillah of Rajshaye.

Inhabitants of Noakhally.
" of the Town and Zillah Barasat.
" of Santipore.
" of Bhowanypore.

The Mohamedan Community of Calcutta.

The Mohamedan Association of Calcutta.

Some of the Native regiments also presented loyal addresses, and with a few exceptions, remained true to their words.

CHAPTER XXXII.

THE BENGALEE'S ADDRESS.

To the Right Hon'ble CHARLES JOHN VISCOUNT CANNING, Governor-General of India, &c., &c.

My Lord,—We, the undersigned Rajahs, Zemindars, Talookdars, Merchants, and other natives of the province of Bengal, take the earliest opportunity, on the retaking of Delhi, to offer your Lordship in Council our warmest congratulations on the signal success which has attended the British arms, under circumstances unparalleled in the annals of British India.

The establishment of British supremacy was considered to have been completely effected a century ago, when Clive led a few ill-trained battalions against the preponderating and well equipped force which represented the Mogul power on the plains of Plassey. But whether the inadequacy of the means or the magnitude of that achievement, were more deserving of admiration, has not yet been determined by history.

No difference of opinion, however, can exist, as to the recapture of Delhi, the details of which have recently been published for general information. Though no one capable of forming a judgment on the subject ever doubted for a moment of the speedy reduction of Delhi, yet some little misgiving might have been felt by those who knew how well furnished was the place with the munitions of war, and occupied by what an immense number of men, whose fiendish animosity was excited to the utmost by that resolution, discipline, and acquaintance with the art of war, which they had acquired by long training in the ranks from which they had basely revolted. But there can be no question of the admiration with which the world will learn by what a handful of men the arduous work has been achieved,—in a brief period,—with the limited resources, a most unlooked for exigency afforded,—and amid discouragements arising from the unhealthiness of the season, that were all but overwhelming.

Such a result under such circumstances never could have been hoped for, but from the well grounded confidence of brave hearts, heroically devoted to the service of their country, and sustained by a sense of hereditary and indomitable prowess.

Happily remote from the scene of the outrages, which have darkened the aspect of the land, and tarnished that reputation for fidelity for which the native soldiery were once pre-eminent, we have derived sincere consolation from the reflection that in Bengal Proper there has been no disturbance, not even a symptom of disaffection ; but that, on the contrary, the people have maintained that loyalty and devotion to the British Government, which led their ancestors to hail, and as far as they could to facilitate, the rising ascendency of that power.

Under the fostering influence of that Government, the population of the country has increased, its agriculture has extended, security has been given to life and property, and the value of land, both at the Presidency and in the interior, has been very considerably enhanced.

Such, indeed, has been the confidence of the people throughout Bengal in the security of the British rule, that these benefits have gone on progressively, even during the height of the disturbances and alarms that have prevailed in the North-Western Provinces.

Sensible of the benefits they have enjoyed under British administration, the people could not but cordially sympathise with the embarrassing position in which their Rulers had suddenly been placed, and sincerely long for the speedy and entire re-establishment of British supremacy in the disturbed districts. So entirely have they identified their interests with those of their Rulers, that the natives of Bengal, men, women, and children have in every part of the scene of the mutinies, been exposed to the same rancour, and treated with the same cruelty, which the mutineers and their misguided countrymen have displayed towards the British within their reach.

While we review with exultation the benefits our countrymen at large have derived from their connection with and steadfast adherence to the British power, and while we congratulate your Lordship in Council on the success of the British arms against the mutinous soldiery, and on the happy prospect before us of the early restoration of tranquillity, we cannot fail to advert, and with no less satisfaction, to the administrative abilities which have conspicuously marked this part of your Lordship's career, and which have indeed been fully equal to the crisis. No sooner had the disloyalty of the Sepoys been distinctly exhibited, than your Lordship took measures, with equal foresight and energy, to obtain reinforcements of British troops, as well from the neighbouring Presidencies and dependencies of the British Crown, as from the expedition then known to be on its way to a wholly different sphere of operations, and to hasten them to the disturbed districts.

Such measures at once assured the public of the speedy restoration of tranquillity throughout these territories. But not satisfied with these prospective advantages, your Lordship made such prompt use of the means that were within your immediate reach at the moment as to ensure the reduction of the stronghold and rallying point of the mutineers, long ere the arrival of any considerable portion of the succours which Her Majesty's Government were prepared to send out to India, for the restoration of this empire to its former condition.

In your anxiety to dispel those clouds which have troubled the political horizon, your Lordship has not been inattentive to measures which would have appeared as of subordinate importance to minds of less perspicacity, foresight, and comprehension. It has been a prominent object with your Lordship both effectually to crush the disaffected and rebellious, and to protect and reassure the loyal and obedient. Accordingly, the extensive powers of legislation vested in your hands have been employed to punish crimes of every form and magnitude against the State with promptitude and rigour; to check vigorously the progress of sedition and disloyalty; and to give a guarantee to the people at large that those powers would be wielded with justice and discrimination, so as to guard as far as possible against faithful and innocent subjects being confounded with the disseminators of sedition and and the perpetrators of open mutiny or secret treachery.

Permit us to hope that your Lordship in Council will receive our heartfelt congratulations on the eminent success which has crowned the British arms, and the warmest expression of our confidence from the opportune display of those signal talents which have distinguished your administration in times of unexampled difficulty and have largely contributed to the safety of the British empire in these regions and the re-assurance of the peaceful and loyal.

We have the honor to be, My Lord,

Your most obedient and faithful servants,

(Signed) MAHARAJAH MAHATAB CHUND BAHADOOR *of Burdwan*,

RAJAH RADHAKANT BAHADOOR,

RAJAH KALIKRISNA BAHADOOR,

And others, inhabitants of Bengal, upwards of Two Thousand Five Hundred.

REPLY.

No. 2699.

FROM CECIL BEADON, ESQ.,

Secretary to the Government of India:

TO MAHARAJAH MAHATAB CHUND BAHADOOR *of Burdwan*, RAJAH RADHAKANT BAHADOOR, RAJAH KALIKRISNA BAHADOOR *and others.*

Dated the 17th December, 1857.

Home Department.

GENTLEMEN,—I am directed by the Right Hon'ble the Governor-General in Council to thank you for your address of congratulation upon the success of the British Arms in the North-Western Provinces.

The honor which you give to the brave men who recaptured Delhi, is richly deserved. The Governor-General in Council agrees with you in believing that when the difficulties and discouragement by which Major-General Wilson and his troops were beset, shall be fully known, their achievement will call forth the admiration of the world.

It is a pleasure to the Governor-General in Council to be able to confirm the praise for unbroken loyalty, which you have claimed for the province of Bengal Proper. Excepting places where the inhabitants have suffered violence from a mutinous soldiery beyond the reach of English troops, there has been no disturbance in that province ; the wealthiest, the most richly cultivated, and the most thickly peopled, of India, and yet the one which for many years past has had least share of protection from European troops.

The Governor-General in Council receives with great satisfaction the expression of your confidence in the Government. No man living have a deeper stake in its measures and its policy than yourselves. If peace, order, and security are valuable to any, they are so to those who, like the foremost amongst you, hold high rank, large hereditary possessions, accumulated wealth, and respected social positions. You do rightly regard your interests, as bound up with those of your rulers, and you may be certain that your rulers will do nothing to sever them. Justice, policy, and the duty of England to India forbid it.

In conclusion, the Governor-General in Council desires me to thank you for the spirit of attachment and loyalty to the British Government, which has dictated your address.

I have the honor to be, &c.,

CECIL BEADON,

Secy. to the Govt. of India.

Fort William,
The 17th Dec., 1857.

CHAPTER XXXIII.

TO THE RIGHT HON'BLE CHARLES JOHN VISCOUNT CANNING, GOVERNOR-GENERAL OF INDIA IN COUNCIL.

MY LORD,—We, the undersigned Rajahs, Zemindars, Talookdars, Merchants, Tradesmen, Agriculturists and other natives of the provinces of Bengal, Behar and Orissa, beg leave to approach your Lordship in Council with this address expressive of our deep sense of gratitude for the several measures of security adopted by your Lordship in Council since disturbances have broken out in the Upper and Central Provinces of British India, and of our admiration for the wisdom, justice and foresight which characterize those measures.

The difficulties which beset the Government of an empire so peculiarly constituted as that of British India, must, under any circumstances, be great and calculated to task the most practised statesmanship. But at a time like this, when the most momentous crisis that can occur in the history of a country is passing over ours, the successsful conduct of affairs ought to entitle those entrusted with the public safety to the most unbounded praise, and to inspire the utmost confidence in their measures.

We, the undersigned, on our part and on the part of our countrymen generally, beg leave most respectfully to affirm that such praise is emphatically due to the administration of which your Lordship is the head, and such confidence is most worthily reposed by your countrymen in its justice, capacity and wisdom.

Such an expression of opinion as we intend this address to be, might, under ordinary circumstances, be liable to be considered as uncalled for, and even, perhaps presumptuous. But under existing circumstances we feel it a duty to our countrymen to adopt the course we have done. It has become notorious throughout this land that your Lordship's administration has been assailed by faction, and assailed because your Lordship in Council has refused compliance with capricious demands, and to treat the loyal portion of the Indian population as rebels, because your Lordship has directed that punishment for offences against the State should be dealt out with discrimination, because your Lordship having regard for the future has not pursued a policy of universal irritation and unreasoning violence, and finally because your Lordship has confined coercion and punishment within necessary and politic limits.

Whatever may be the motives that influenced those who have joined in these proceedings, we entertain no apprehensions whatever of their representations having the effect which they desire to produce. We have observed with pain, but without misgiving, the incessant, though happily harmless, endeavours made by them to thwart the action of authority, to impeach its views and to embarrass its councils. But now that, My Lord, they have ventured to carry their misstatements to the foot of the Throne, it is time,—and justice to ourselves and to our countrymen demands,—that a national protest against these most unjustifiable proceedings should be thus placed upon record.

We beg permission to subscribe ourselves,

My Lord,

Your Lordship's most obedient and faithful servants,

(Signed) MAHARAJAH SREESH CHUNDER ROY,

And more than 5,000 natives of the Provinces of Bengal, Behar and Orissa.

REPLY

No. 2700.

From CECIL BEADON, Esq.,

Secretary to the Government of India,

To MAHARAJAH SREESH CHUNDER BAHADOOR, *Of Nuddeah,*

RAJAH PERTAUB CHUNDER SING BAHADOOR,

" PRASONONATH ROY BAHADOOR,

BABOO JOYKISSEN MOOKERJEE, *and others.*

Dated the 17th December, 1857.

Home Department.

GENTLEMEN,—The Right Hon'ble the Governor-General in Council directs me to thank you for the address which he has received at your hands.

The Governor-General in Council sees amongst the numerous signatures to that address the names of men of ancient lineage, of vast possessions, and of great wealth; of men of cultivated intelligence, who have been foremost in measures of beneficence in the encouragement of education, and in works of material public improvement; men whose influence with their fellow-countrymen is deservedly great, and whose interest in the peace and well-being of India, it would be difficult to exaggerate.

No person will hold cheaply the opinions of such a body, and the possession of its confidence and good will would be a source of strength to any Government.

Therefore the Governor-General in Council desires me, in thanking you for your address, to add emphatically that he receives it with much satisfaction.

The motives which have induced the presentation of the address are stated by you. Upon these the Governor-General in Council desires me to say a few words.

In times of heat and violence, when the hearts of individuals have been torn, and the feelings of classes inflamed, the judgment which men pass upon each other and upon events around them are seldom dispassionate; especially their judgments upon those whose high and solemn duty it is, whilst repressing crime and averting danger, to guide the measures of the State in the straight path of justice.

In such times there lies upon every loyal man the obligation so to govern his acts and words so as to prevent or allay irritation; not to excite or heighten it. The Governor-General in Council calls upon you, each in your sphere, to be mindful of this duty.

The Governor-General in Council wishes you to rest assured that the Government of India will not forget, that England will not forget that if unhappily the mutineers and rebels of India are to be reckoned by thousands, the peaceful and loyal subjects of the Queen in India are numbered by millions. You may be sure that by no act of the Government, by no general proscriptions or sweeping condemnations of race or creed, shall these last men be classed with the first.

The course of the Government of India has been, and will continue to be simple and clear · to strike down resistance without mercy ; but when resistance ends to allow deliberate justice to resume its sway ; justice stern and inflexible, but patient and discriminating.

I have the honor to be, Gentlemen,

Your most obedient servant,

(Sd.) CECIL BEADON,

Secy. to the Govt. of India.

Fort William 17*th Dec.*, 1857.

CHAPTER XXXIV.

WE take the following remarks from the *Times* on the foregoing addresses as expressive of English opinion in respect to them :—

" The gentry, the landowners and the capitalists of Bengal and the neighbouring provinces have not been insensible to the prudent impartiality of Lord Canning's language and conduct. In two well-written addresses they have thanked him for his resistance to the clamour against the natives and congratulated him on the success of the English arms at Delhi. More than 2,000 memorialists remind Government of the fact, often stated in our own correspondence that "the natives of Bengal men, women, and children—have, in every part of the scene of the mutinies, been exposed to the same rancour and treated with the same cruelty which the mutineers and their misguided countrymen have displayed towards the British within their reach." They recognized as equal merits the determination to crush the disaffected and rebellious, and the resolution to protect and reassure the loyal and obedient. Every civil and military official, every soldier, almost every Englishman, may claim to share the credit of the vigour wcich has been displayed, the honor of steadily discriminating between the rebels and the peaceful community is assigned by the common voice of bitter enemies and of ardent friends principally to the Governor-General. Another memorial bearing 5,000 signatures more directly refers to the demands put forth in the well known Calcutta petition. "It has become notorious," it is said, "throughout this land that your Lordship's Administration has been assailed by faction, and assailed because your

Lordship in Council has refused compliance with capricious demands, and to treat the loyal portion of the Indian population as rebels: because your Lordship has directed that punishment for offences against the state should be dealt out with discrimination; because your Lordship having regard for the future has not pursued a policy of universal irritation and unreasoning violence; and finally, because your Lordship has confined coercion and punishment within necessary and politic limits."

The importance of such declarations by no means depends on the justice of the reasoning or the accuracy of the statements which they contain. The Calcutta Opposition will probably complain that the wishes and opinions of suspected aliens should be placed in competition with their own; but the Government of India, after all, ought to remember that its subjects are principally Indians. Rajahs and Zemindars, Talookdars and Merchants may possibly be perfidious and are certainly heterodox; but it would be inconvenient if their influence over their countrymen was employed to embarrass the Government. According to one familiar test of respectability the memorialists may well be thought entitled to courtesy and consideration. Their collective wealth would probably buy up Lombard Street; the extent of their landed estates might in some instances be admired even by an English Duke.

One of the gentlemen who sign the address represents the ancient Hindoo dynasty, which reigned in Southern Bengal before the Mahomedan conquest. The Moharajah of Burdwan pays land revenue to the amount of more than half a million sterling a year. A Rajah with an unpronounceable name at one time subscribed £5,000 to the Native Hospital. Another has founded between 40 and 50 schools. Shamachurn Mullick's loyalty may perhaps be partially explained by the statement that he is the largest holder of Government promissory notes in Bengal; but every serious politician will admit that the wealthy leaders of a highly civilized society are worth conciliating, especially when they simply demand justice and protection to which they are entitled.

It may be said that the Brahmin Sepoys were as smooth and plausible as the members of their caste at Calcutta; but the question is not whether the Bengalese should be armed and drilled. The Government is not responsible for their existence or social position, and it is placed there for the very purpose of securing to them peace and justice. Five years since there was a premature clamour for the advancement of natives to high offices in the administration. The opposite demand, that their interests and feelings should be sacrificed to the claims of a superior race, will be even more transitory. The experiment in which Lord Canning has refused his co-operation was tried long since in Central and Southern America. Two ancient, though inferior, forms of civilization were rudely trampled out by the conquerors of Mexico and of Peru. The Spaniards put themselves in the place not of the Government, but of the nation, and exercised their power ostensibly as well as really for the exclusive benefit of the dominant race; but from that time to the present day they have degenerated towards the level of the subject population which they had at first degraded. The English Government of India has undertaken the nobler task of wielding the sceptre of Akbar and of Baber for the benefit of the native population as well as of their conquerors. The interests of England are best promoted by the prosperity of her Imperial dependency, and by the gradual elevation of the Indian races to a higher standard of civilization. The Governor-General has understood this true policy of his country; and, if he has occasionally seemed to incline too much to a system of conciliation, it must be remembered that his error was on the side of prudence and that he had not only to suppress the mutiny but in doing so *not* to render our future tenure of India impossible."—*Times*, *Feb.* 4.

We republish the above addresses of confidence in the Administration and the remarks of the *Times* thereon without comment. The doings of the "Calcutta Malcontents" in the way of enhancing the difficulties and helping the continuance of the struggle by irritating race-prejudices and fostering race-hatreds are notorious, and the remarkably good temper, calm courage, grasping mind and unerring instinct displayed by Lord Canning and his Council in resisting what M. Montalembert in his celebrated *Debate on India* calls the "hateful promptings and sanguinary incitements" of the independent British community here, have become equally famous to call for especial remark. But we may be permitted to observe that while the character of our countrymen was being most foully calumniated, and the bitterest aspersions were being made on them as members of society,—that while a series of legislative measures was passed, untying to a very serious extent the joint of social tranquillity and happiness, which have been justly characterized by a remarkable writer in a remarkable article * in the last

* A DISTRICT DURING A REBELLION, *Calcutta Review*, No. LXI. This is one of those papers which will elucidate

number of the *Calcutta Review*, as "unequalled since that of Draco, for every line is written in blood, and all protection to life, liberty and property was removed"—that while hundreds of their fellow-countrymen were perishing violently, without enquiry and with no formality of justice, and blood was most recklessly being shed, which to quote the same feeling writer, "which the waters of the Ganges will not wash and the memory of which years will not efface"—that in the midst of this revolutionary storm, calculated to uproot the deep-seated affections of the most cool-tempered people, the leaders of our society,—conscious of their position from the mistaken hostility of the Sepoys and of the good-will of the higher class of the European community here, and of the earnestness and anxiety of the Supreme Government to see justice done and the usual tone of the state machinery restored,—publicly and with perfect cheerfulness offered their good wishes to the success and prosperity of the British cause,

to the future historian of the Indian revolt some of its gloomiest features.—*Compiler.*

expressing their highest confidence in the Administration, and this at the time when its acts were calumniated and impeached. What effects these demonstrations have achieved are signally marked by the increasing intelligence displayed by the British public in appreciating Lord Canning's policy and measures. Bigoted and hostile Contemporaries may impugn the motives and trifle with the aim of these loyalists, but the future historian of the revolt will, we confidently hope, do them justice.

We will conclude this part of our labors with one more instance. Here is a testimony to the conduct of the general body of Bengali Uncovenanted Servants in the North-West accorded by a worthy eye-witness, we mean the writer in the *Calcutta Review* quoted above. "Be it recorded (says the Reviewer) to the honor of the Natives of Bengal Proper who have monopolized the English offices in the North-Western Provinces, that timid and pusillanimous as they notoriously are, NO ONE INSTANCE OF THEIR HAVING FAILED IN LOYALTY IS ON RECORD."

The public has of late heard much of the "Fighting Moonsiff." The Reviewer thus speaks of him :—

"In one remarkable instance the native Civil Judge—a Bengal Baboo by capacity and valor—brought himself so conspicuously forward, as to be known as "the fighting Moonsiff." He not only held his own defiantly, but he planned attacks, he burnt villages, he wrote English despatches thanking his subordinates, and displayed a capacity for rule and a fertility of resource very remarkable for one of his nation."*

We gather from the *Hindoo Patriot* that this native gentleman is Baboo Pearymohun Banerjee of the Woterparah Banerjees. He was educated at first in the Woterparah school and afterwards in the

---

*The *Friend of India* calls the last two lines the offspring of a "laughable prejudice." "We are not slow (says the *Friend*,) to scold Bengalees when required, but if in India there is a race to whom God has given capacity, real clearness of brain, it is the Bengalee. Take the most timid, quaking wretch or a Kayust you can find, put him in any district in India with a shadow of authority, and if he does not make Punjabee and Sikh, Marhatta and Hindostanee, work themselves to death for his benefit, and think all the while it is for their own, he is no true Bengalee."—*Compiler.*

Hindoo College. He was Moonsiff of Allahabad at the time of the Mutiny. As an acknowledgment of his valorous and conspicuous services he has been made Deputy Magistrate and Deputy Collector of Banda."

STATEMENTS OF NATIVE FIDELITY EXHIBITED DURING THE MUTINIES OF 1857-58.

Place.	*Person.*	*Authority.*	*Services.*
Secunderabad.........	The troops of the 2nd Cavalry, Hydrabad Contingent, and the Resildar.	*Madras Spectator*, July 25, quoted by the *Bengal Hurkaru*, August 11, 1858.	The troops of the 2nd Cavalry of Hydrabad Contingent, which was in guard at the Residency behaved most gallantly during the whole affair. (The repulsing the attack of a Rohillah body.) The conduct of the Resildar was so conspicuous, exposing himself as he did to find out all that was going on, that it is understood that the Resident was resolved to promote him.—*Madras Spectator, July* 25, 1858.
Gopalparah.......	The Rajah of Gopalparah.	*Hurkaru*, June 27, 1858.	An Officer of the 22nd Regiment which mutinied at Fyzabad, after stating the inconveniences he with others was put to thereby, writes to the *Hurkaru*: "The Rajah has taken compassion on us here, and is going to send us to Dinapore."
Mhow.......	The Native Officer of the 23rd Native Infantry.	*Mofussilite*, June 16, quoted by the *Hurkaru*, July 8, 1858.	A budmash attempted to incite the Sepoys stating that the European Artillery were ready to fire and blow them away. The Native Officer of the 23rd Native Infantry refused him ingress into the place where the arms were and stopped him. The writer in the *Mofussilite* adds, "it has gone abroad that the Commanding Officer of Artillery saved a rise, but it is no such thing, it was the Native Officer's fidelity and pluck that did it."

STATISTICS OF NATIVE FIDELITY EXHIBITED DURING THE MUTINIES OF 1857-58.

Place.	*Person.*	*Authority.*	*Services.*
Budaun...	Newab Ahmud Yar Khan.	*Mofussilite*, June 16, quoted by the *Hurkaru*, July 9, 1858.	The fugitives from Budaun were cordially received and hospitably entertained by the Newab.
Marwar...	Maharajah Tukhut Sing of Marwar.	*Hurkaru*, July 14, 1858.	The *Hurkaru* writes: "We have been informed that besides some of the Rajpoot chiefs, Maharajah Tukhut Sing of Marwar, has promised to send two thousand cavalry sowars and as many infantry men with an adequate number of Sirdars or officers to aid the British Government in quelling the insurrection of the sepoys."
Serampore and Calcutta.......	The Gossaines of Serampore and Baboo Samachurn Mullick.......	*Hurkaru*, July 18, 1858.	The rich Gossaines of Serampore offered some of their houses for the accommodation of soldiers free of cost to Government. Baboo Shama Churn Mullick, a rich millionaire of Calcutta, also offered his splendid mansion meeting the Chitpore Road for the accommodation of the Hindu School, when the Hindu School building was occupied by newly arrived soldiers.
Fyzabad...	Maun Sing of Oude.	*Hurkaru*, July 21, 1858.	Mrs. Busher, Mrs. Matthews, and Mr. Edwards with lots of children were rescued from Fyzabad by Maun Sing.

STATEMENTS OF NATIVE FIDELITY EXHIBITED DURING THE MUTINIES OF 1857-58.

Place.	*Person.*	*Authority.*	*Services.*
Cawnpore..	The Subadar of the Cawnpore Regiment.	*Bombay Times*, July 10, quoted by the *Hurkaru*, July 22, 1858.	The Agra correspondent of the *Bombay Times* states that when the sepoys mutinied at Cawnpore, the Subadar lost his life in attempting to protect the Treasury.
"	The Rampore Newab.	*Ibid.*	The same writer says: "It is related on tolerably good authority that when the 29th native Infantry were passing the Rampore Jageer on their way to Bareilly, the Rampore Newab disarmed them and took from them all the treasure. The same Newab, it is said, assisted English refugees at Nyne Tal with supplies.
Nuzufghur.	The Rajah of Nuzufghur.	*Hurkaru*, September 5, 1858.	One of the survivors of the Cawnpore massacre, after describing the celebrated Boat episode says, "when we had got down about 6 miles, firing on both sides ceased, and soon after we were hailed by some on the Oude side who asked us to come on shore, and said they would take us to their Rajah who was friendly to the English. We gave ourselves up and were taken six miles in land to the Rajah who treated us very kindly, giving us food and clothes. We stayed with him for about a month but he would not let us leave, saying the roads were unsafe."

STATEMENTS OF NATIVE FIDELITY EXHIBITED DURING THE MUTINIES OF 1857-58.

Place.	*Person.*	*Authority.*	*Services.*
Agra.......	The Hindoos of the City.	*Hurkaru*, September 8, 1858.	The writer says "the Hindoos seem to cling to us and however come down with loans to Government."
Fyzabad....	A sepoy of the 21st Native Infantry.	*Ibid.*	The sepoy communicated to the writer who was an officer of the Regiment, of the designs of his comrades and thereby saved the lives of some of the Europeans of the station.
"	An inhabitant.	*Ibid.*	This inhabitant served as a guide to a party of fugitives from Fyzabad.
"	The Rajah of Gopalpore.	*Ibid.*	The writer says that in course of their journey the above party of fugitives reached the place of the Rajah of Gopalpore who treated them like gentlemen, gave them food and clothing, and offered them money and most other things which they required.
Bhagulpore.........	The people of Bhagulpore.	*Ibid.*	The party were next served by the people of Bhagulpore.
Kolapore...	Two Havildars of the 27th Regt.	*Bombay Telegraph and Courier* quoted by the *Hurkaru*, September 10, 1858.	These Havildars escorted Mr. Rolland across the country to the Residency.

STATEMENTS OF NATIVE FIDELITY EXHIBITED DURING THE MUTINIES OF 1857-58.

Place.	*Person.*	*Authority.*	*Services.*
Kolapore..	The Rajah of Kolapore.	*Bombay Telegraph and Courier.*	In the suppression of the outbreak at Kolapore, the Rajah assisted Col. Maughan and lent him three guns.
Sealkote....	Sepoy Bhowany Sing.	*Ibid.*	This Sepoy escorted European children from Sealkote on the occurrence of the outbreak there.
"	Sooban Khan Havildar and two troopers.	*Ibid.*	The Subadar and Troopers escorted to the Fort, Col. Campbell, his wife, Mrs. Graham, the widow of Dr. C. Graham, Mr. Gray and the children.
"	A trooper.	*Ibid.*	Escorted Miss Graham, the daughter of the Superintending Surgeon.
Sealkote....	Tilluck Pandy..	*Bombay Telegraph and Courier*, quoted by the *Hurkaru*, September 10, 1858.	"This was an extraordinary Act of fidelity. When the mutiny first broke out, the Soobadar of the guard was asked by several men to join it which he declined but subsequently finding the rising general, they (the guard) all went off after helping themselves to ammunition. One sepoy alone, Tilluck Pandy, on some pretence remained behind and stationed himself at the Quarter Guard, where he seems to have been left undisturbed till the afternoon when two troopers and one khalasee came to explode the magazine. Tilluck Pandy told them not to

Place.	*Person.*	*Authority.*	*Services.*
Sealkote....	Tilluck Pandy.	*Bombay Telegraph and Courier*, quoted by the *Hurkaru*, September 10, 1858.—(*Continued.*)	trouble themselves about that, as he had remained there for that purpose and would do it, whereupon they went away to the Artillery magazine which soon after blew up in a dense black cloud. Tilluck Pandy was no more disturbed, except by villagers whom he frightened by pointing his musket towards them, and when the first party (Europeans) from the Fort came into cantonments, the next morning this faithful Pandy was found guarding his post. It was afterwards discovered that he had thus saved in the magazine 80,000 ball cartridges, nearly as many caps, the clothing of the regiment and much officers' property and "messplate."
"	The washerman of Major Drake and his wife.	*Ibid.*	Protected Major Drake's property.
Meean Meer.	The Havildar Major, the Pay Havildar and a few others of the 26th Regiment Local Infantry.	*Mofussilite*, Aug. 11, quoted by *Hurkaru*, Sept. 17, 1858.	Lost their lives in attempting to maintain order among their regiment.

STATEMENTS OF NATIVE FIDELITY EXHIBITED DURING THE MUTINIES OF 1857-58.

Place.	*Person.*	*Authority.*	*Services.*
Comillah...	Baboo Bungshee Lochun Mitter.	*Hurkaru*, December 7, 1858.	When the mutineers in Eastern Bengal advanced towards Tipperah, the Judge and other Christian inhabitants with their wives and children were housed, fed and protected by Baboo Bungsee Lochun Mitter, who entertained for their protection a guard of about forty Burkundazes. The Baboo afterwards escorted the party to Dacca.
Some Village near Chirkaree.	Some Brahmin Zemindar.	*Hurkaru*, November 10, 1858.	Offered shelter and protection to Mr. H. V Sturt.
Cherkaree.	The Rajah of place.	*Ibid.*	Ditto.
Calcutta...	Baboo Sreekissen Sing.	*Hurkaru*, November 25, 1858.	As a token of his loyalty offered a present to Government of a large and beautiful elephant for the service of the State.
Singhbhoom	Rajah of Serakhillah and the Thakoor of Khersherwah.	*Hurkaru*, November 27, 1858.	Offered personal services and a supply of some 700 or 800 retainers.

STATEMENTS OF NATIVE FIDELITY EXHIBITED DURING THE MUTINIES OF 1857-58.

Place.	*Person.*	*Authority.*	*Services.*
Bhooloah...	Baboo Joshoda Coomer Pyne, the Naib of the Rajahs Pertaup Chunder and Issur Chunder Sings, Zemindars of Bhooloah.	*Hurkaru*, December 5, 1858.	The newswriter writes, "The news of the outbreak at Chittagong, on the night of the 19th, reached the Authorities here at about 10½ P. M. on the night of the following day by Express Dak. That very moment the Magistrate accompanied by Mr. Peacock, proceeded to the strong-built cutchery house of the Zemindars of Bhooloah, Rajahs Pertaup Chunder and Issur Chunder Sings of Calcutta, and after a consultation with their able and well-informed naib or agent Baboo Joshoda Coomar Pyne, ordered him immediately to collect there a body of fighting lattials with sufficient quantities of food, and issued Purwannahs or orders on the Police Darogahs and employed horsemen to bring intelligence of the movements of the enemy. The activity and zeal with which these orders were performed may be understood, when I inform you that the very next day a body of five hundred fighting men with arms in their hands, was collected in and around the cutchery house referred to, while another body of more than that number were divided into parties and located at the most favourable points along the road leading to Sodharum, &c., &c.

STATEMENTS OF NATIVE FIDELITY EXHIBITED DURING THE MUTINIES OF 1857-58.

Place.	*Person.*	*Authority.*	*Services.*
Patna.........	The late Nazir of Patna.	P. P. E. I. Mutinies, No. 7.	"The late Nazir of Patna had by his exertions contributed much to this state of things (restoration of tranquillity) and had sent in a large number of prisoners." Narrative of events by A. R. Young, Esquire, Secretary to the Government of Bengal, dated October 10th, 1857.
Paneehatee.	Baboos Prankissen Roy Chowdry and Juggut Chunder Roy Chowdry, Zemindars of Paneehatee.	Appendix P. P. E. I. Mutinies, No. 5.	Explained to the people of their zemindarees (about 50,000 in number) the Govt. Proclamation, dated 16th May, 1857, assuring them that Govt. never interfered or intended to interfere with their religious beliefs and customs, and exhorted them to loyalty by setting forth the advantages the country has derived from the British rule.
Hazareebag.	Teeluck Das of Nyaghur and the Rajah of Talchere & Koenghur.	P. P. E. I. Mutinies, No. 7.	Arrested and sent in certain convicts and prisoners.
Ramghur...	The Zemindar of Ramghur...	*Ibid.*	Acted on behalf of the British Government.

Statements of Native Fidelity exhibited during the Mutinies of 1857-58.

Place.	*Person.*	*Authority.*	*Services.*
Sahabad...	Maharajah Mohessur Buksh Sing.	P. P. E. I. Mutinies, No. 7.	Assisted the Government with men and money.
Behar......	Some Zemindars.	*Ibid.*	Aided the Government with the amount of their revenues in gold coins and sicca rupees, though they could not collect their rents from their ryots.
Patna......	Rajah Bhoop Sing.	*Ibid.*	Aided the Government and continued in his loyal services.
Sarun......	Maharajah Chutterdharee Sahage Bahadoor.	*Ibid.*	Took active measures on behalf of the British Government.
Singhbhoom	Native Officers of the Sen. Asst. Comis. Office.	*Ibid.*	Rendered loyal services.
Beerbhoom and Manbhoom......	Zemindars of Beerbhoom and Manbhoom.	*Ibid.*	Assisted Government in the restoration of order. The following zemindars also rendered the same services. Mokundonarain Deo of Manbhoom, Raja Radakisto Deo of Burrabhoom, Raja Sutroghun Deo, zemindars of Patcom, Rajah Reegonauth Sing, zemindar of Hogmondee, and the zemindar of Saelpore, Rajah Chuttrepur Deo of Ghasellah.

STATEMENTS OF NATIVE FIDELITY EXHIBITED DURING THE MUTINIES OF 1857-58.

Place.	*Person.*	*Authority.*	*Services.*
Santipore...	Baboo Issur Chunder Ghossal, Deputy Magistrate.	P. P. E. I. Mutinies No. 7.	Offered himself to go anywhere for the service of Govt. and received thanks for the same.
Behar......	Shah Kerbeer Oddeen Ahmed.	*Ibid.*	Rendered various services to Government, and proved of especial usefulness on the rising of Koero Sing at Arrah.
Kalabundv.	Sree Adit Pertaub Deo.	*Ibid.*	Ditto.
Moorshedabad.	The Newab of Moorshidabad.	*Ibid.*	Stood firm in his attachment to British Government and rendered good services.
Jawnpore.	Ramprosad Sing.	*Ibid.*	Sheltered and protected the Europeans who fled from Cawnpore and rendered other loyal services.
Mynpooree	Bhowany Singh Rao.	*Ibid.*	Rendered services to Government.
Futtehghur.	A Brahmin.	*Ibid.*	Sheltered and protected a fugitive from Futtehghur.
Cawnpore.	Moonshee Sheopershad.	*Ibid.*	Exerted himself conspicuously on behalf of the British Government under great personal difficulties.

STATEMENTS OF NATIVE FIDELITY EXHIBITED DURING THE MUTINIES OF 1857-58.

Place.	*Person.*	*Authority.*	*Services.*
Jalaun....	The Rajah of Samptur.	P. P. E. I. Mutinies, No. 7.	Supplied the Deputy Commissioner of Jalaun with a great number of men, guns and ammunition.
Bhind....	A faithful servant.	*Ibid.*	Saved the lives of a number of European fugitives by preventing them from proceeding to Gwalior.
Benares...	Hingun Laul late Tehsildar of Derra Dhoon.	*Ibid.*	Saved the lives of Mr. France and his party and restored order in Pergunnah Keerakut.
Chuprah...	Ramzan Ali.	*Ibid.*	Mr. Samuells, the Commissioner of Patna, says "Had it not been for his exertions the same scenes would have followed the abandonment of the station of Chuprah as were exhibited on a similar occasion at Gaya."
Sewan....	Mahomed Wajed.	*Ibid.*	Kept order at Sewan in conjunction with the Hutwa Rajah.
Muzufferpore.......	Baboo Nundulaul Mohtoe.	*Ibid.*	Exerted himself most conspicuously for the preservation of order.

STATEMENTS OF NATIVE FIDELITY EXHIBITED DURING THE MUTINIES OF 1857-58.

Place.	*Person.*	*Authority.*	*Services.*
Muzuffer-pore.......	Hydur Buksh	P. P. E. I. Mutinies, No. 7.	Rendered good services to Government.
Ditto.......	Mohes Lall.	*Ibid.*	Was recommended for a reward of Rs. 200 in consideration of his loyal services.
Ditto.......	Mohamed Tokee.	*Ibid.*	Was staunch and rendered some service to Government.
Sewan. ...	Burrowley & Luchmon Sahoye.	*Ibid.*	Saved Messrs. Lynch and Donell.
Ditto.......	Errayut Hossein.	*Ibid.*	Rendered good services to Government.
Ditto.......	Shah Khyrut and Ahmed Hossein.	*Ibid.*	Offered protection to European fugitives.
Jahanabad.	Mohamed Furreedoodeen, Moonsiff.	*Ibid.*	Preserved order.
Bhagul-pore.......	Rajah Jymunt Sing.	*Ibid.*	Rendered material assistance to the authorities.
Ditto.......	Mahinder-narain of Geddhour.	*Ibid.*	Behaved himself creditably.

STATEMENTS OF NATIVE FIDELITY EXHIBITED DURING THE MUTINIES OF 1857-58.

Place.	*Person.*	*Authority.*	*Services.*
Bhaugulpore	Fetah Ali Khan Zemindar of Sheekhpoor.	P. P. E. I. Mutineis, No. 7.	Assisted Government.
Ditto......	Mahomed Rajah.	*Ibid.*	Exerted himself loyally.
Benares...	Lall Bunkey Laul.	*Ibid.*	Rendered loyal services.
Dacca....	Zemindars.	*Ibid.*	Messrs. Anund Kissore Roy and Ram Chunder of Mymensing, and Moulvie Ally and Moulvie Rajah Abdool Gunney of Dacca, supplied Government with elephants, &c., free of cost.
Maghubee.	The Rajah of Maghubee.	*Ibid.*	Rendered loyal services.
Singramon.	Rundhur Sing.	*Ibid.*	Afforded assistance to Government.
Purneah.	The Rajah of Purneah.	*Ibid.*	Was staunch and rendered loyal services.
Kuttinque.	Havildar Hatta Tewarree, and Privates Ram Churn and Sheik Oman.	*Ibid.*	Rendered conspicuous and gallant services.

STATEMENTS OF NATIVE FIDELITY EXHIBITED DURING THE MUTINIES OF 1857-58.

Place.	*Person.*	*Authority.*	*Services.*
Behar....	Several Rajahs and landholders.	P. P. E. I. Mutinies, No. I	The following Rajahs and landholders are described by the Patna Commissioner, to have vied with each other in the display of their loyalty. Rajahs of Bettiahee Hutwah, Sera Khillah, and Ramghur and Rajah Joymungul Sing and Shah Kulbeeroodeen.
Punnah ...	Maharajah of Punnah.	*Ibid.*	The Fort Kullengur was recovered from the rebels entirely by the zeal, loyalty and good judgment of the Maharajah.
Hazareebag.	Some Officers.	*Ibid.*	These men remained staunch and assisted the commander when their comrades had mutinied.
Fyzabad....	Dhulleep Sing, Subadar of the 28th N. I.	*Ibid.*	This man though he was forced to join his rebellious comrades, still exerted himself conspicuously for the safety of Col. Lennox and other officers of the regiment.
Ditto....	The Nazim of Gorruckpore and his nephew.	*Ibid.*	Sheltered and protected the party of Col. Lennox and contrived every possible means for their safety in which they happily succeeded.
Ditto....	Teg Alllkhan.	*Ibid.*	Assisted a party of Fyzabad fugitives.

STATEMENTS OF NATIVE FIDELITY EXHIBITED DURING THE MUTINIES OF 1857-58

Place.	*Person.*	*Authority.*	*Services.*
Fyzabad...	A village Jamadar.	P P E. I. .Mutinies, No. 7.	Assisted a party of Fyzabad fugitives.
Ditto......	A Tuhsildar.	*Ibid.*	Afforded protection to the party and supplied them with money.
Ditto......	A Brahmin.	*Ibid.*	Afforded shelter and protection to Serjeant Busher, a fugitive from Fyzabad.
Ditto......	Brother of the rebel Bully Sing.	*Ibid.*	Interceded with Bully Sing for the life of Busher and succeeded.
Banda...	The Newab of Banda.	*Ibid.*	Afforded protection to Christian fugitives and supplied them with money.
Rubrai...	An old and retired Subadar.	*Ibid.*	We gather from a letter of Capt. Scott to Major Reid that this Subadar and a retired Native officer did good service during the crisis.
Perneah...	The Rajah of	*Ibid.*	Rendered loyal services to Government by furnishing the authorities with men and supplies, &c.
Agra and Banda...	Subadar Utter Sing and Uttun Sing of the Shik Battalion.	*Ibid.*	Rendered distinguished and gallant services.

STATEMENTS OF NATIVE FIDELITY EXHIBITED DURING THE MUTINIES OF 1857-58.

Place.	*Person.*	*Authority.*	*Services.*
Bettiah...	The Rajah of	P. P. E. I. Mutinies, No. 7.	Assisted the British Government and acted on its behalf.
Allyghur...	Rajah Thackoor Govind Sing.	*Ibid.*	Ditto.
Ghatiapore Pergunnah	Beharee Sing.	*Ibid.*	Mr. Sherer to Mr. Muir, "Order was preserved at Ghatiapore Pergunnah through the exertions and firmness of Behary Sing and others."
Behar......	The Rajah of Durbangha.	*Ibid.*	The late Commissioner of Patna says, "The Rajah of Durbangha offered assistance and the more respectable natives of the town showed a disposition to aid and support the authorities. Rugunundon Sing has offered 30 Rupees for the apprehension of each mutineer and deserter. Chumun Chund Day 15 Rs. and Bagbehary 10 Rs."
Tekaree...	Baboo Mohendi Narain.	*Ibid.*	Assisted the authorities.
Behar......	Rajah Jay Perkas Sing	Appendix P. P. E. I. Mutinies No. 5.	Ditto.

STATEMENTS OF NATIVE FIDELITY EXHIBITED DURING THE MUTINIES OF 1857-58.

Place.	*Person.*	*Authority.*	*Services.*
Muzuffer-pore......	Fuzl Hug.	Appendix P. P. E. I. Mutinies, No. 5,	Assisted the authorities.
Ramghur...	Cowar Ram Sing.	*Ibid.*	Ditto.
Arungabad.	Jhumum Laul and two Chowkeydars.	*Ibid.*	These persons protected the station in the absence of all Civil Officers.
Tirhoot......	Moonshe Iradut Ally.	*Ibid.*	Rendered loyal services to Government.
Agra.........	Thesildars, Thannadars.	*Englishman*, 6th Jan. 1858	Assisted Captain Alexander in his attempt to escape to Agra (received handsome reward from Government.)
Saugor......	200 men 31st Regt.	Saugor Correspondent of the *Englishman*, 6th Jan 1858.	Detachment of 200 men under Capt. Finch, 31st Regiment Native Infantry, advanced and took the Town Bopyle from the mutineers amidst heavy fire.
Luthern-wallah......	Jamar.	*Moffusilite*, Dec. 4, quoted by the *Englishman* of 6th Jan. 1858.	Protected Serjeant Callow & Jarvis on their perilous escape from Sepree.

STATEMENTS OF NATIVE FIDELITY EXHIBITED DURING THE MUTINIES OF 1857-58.

Place.	*Person.*	*Authority.*	*Services.*
Joypore...	Rajah of	*Moffusilite*, quoted by *Englishman*, 9th Jan., 1858.	Assisted the Government on the application of the Political Agent Capt. W. F. Edens, in quelling the disturbed district of Goorgaon. The troops he furnished were also entrusted with the escorting of a number of English Officers, women and children, from Nusseerabad to Agra.
Bousie......	Rajah of	Service Message vide *Englishman*, Jan. 11. 1858.	Intercepted a party who attempted to escape towards Oude.
Nepaul......	Guardsmen of the Resident of Nepaul.	*Englishman*, Jan. 15, 1858.	Apprehended three disaffected persons who had been attempting to tamper with and excite the men to acts of insubordination, (received from Government a reward of Rs. 1,000.)
Gopaulpore.	Rajah of	Gorruckpore Correspondent of the *Englishman* 27th January, 1858.	Captured the Rebel Mushrufkhan and his Companions.
Petturia in the district of Chota Nagpur ...	Preonauth Jogul Paul.	*Englishman*, Jan. 28, 1858.	Government invested him with a Khelat, a life pension of 313 Rupees per annum and the title of Roy Bahadur for the devotedness he evinced to the cause of the British Government during the disturbances.

STATEMENTS OF NATIVE FIDELITY EXHIBITED DURING THE MUTINIES OF 1857-58.

Place.	*Person.*	*Authority.*	*Services.*
Lucknow ...	Old Subadar of the 13th Regiment.	*Englishman*, Jan. 28th, 1858.	Remained attached to a fugitive Captain and interceded for his safety with the rebel sepoys.
Cachar......	Kookies and Ryots and especially a Kookie Chief, named Manjeehows.	*Englishman*, Feb. 2nd, 1858.	Rendered useful services by attacking the mutineers in the jungles.
Sekawatees.	Sekawatee.	*Englishman*, 2nd Feb. 1858.	Behaved most gallantly.
Goonda......	Rajah of	*Englishman* 10th Feb. 1858. Service Message.	Under him the Goorkhas attacked the enemy ten thousand strong.
Bustee.	Mabon Singh.	*Englishman*, Feb. 11, 1858.	Mr. William Osborne, sub-deputy opium agent, says that Maunsing lately saved several Christian fugitives from Lucknow. The fugitives say that Maunsing treated them with every consideration.

STATEMENTS OF NATIVE FIDELITY EXHIBITED DURING THE MUTINIES OF 1857-58.

Place.	*Person.*	*Authority.*	*Services.*
Gopeegunge	A Pundit.	*Englishman*, 17th Feb. 1858.	Saved a certain Government treasure.
Cherkari...	Rajah of	*Englishman*, 18th Service Message.	Through his assistance Mr. Carne, Deputy Collector of Punna, who was shut up with the Rajah in the fort of Cherkari—was able to effect his escape on the 7th March 1858.
Mooshabags, Darogah......	Meer Maped Ally.	*Englishman*, 22nd March, 1858, Service Message.	Gave shelter to 10 Europeans with whom he was subsequently captured by the Calpee rebels.
Tirhoot......	Rajah Joymungal Sing & other Zemindars.	*Englishman*, 9th Apl., 1858.	Rendered distinguished services to Government.
Benares.....	Soorut Singh.	*Englishman*, 17th March, 1858.	Received from the Government for himself and his legitimate heirs (male) an allowance in perpetuity of 400 Rupees per month, and a Khillut of 5,000 Rs.

Statements of Native Fidelity exhibited during the Mutinies of 1857-58.

Place.	*Person.*	*Authority.*	*Services.*
Benares......	Takoor Buldeo Singh.	*Englishman*, 25th J[illegible]858.	Received from Government for conspicuous services a reward of certain confiscated land worth 1,000 Rs. per annum, rent free.
Madhopore Basgareeah Ghaut......	200 Zemindars.	*Englishman*, 10th July, 1858.	Raised people to withstand the rebels. A correspondent of the *Englishman* from Mozufferpore thus speaks of them:— " Were it not for the demonstration made by these men, it is more than probable that Tirhoot would have been infested with the presence of the Mutineers."
Resteet.....,	Zemindar.	*Englishman*, 12th Dec. 1858.	Drove out the rebels.
Simlah	Oozurkhan.	*Englishman*, 15th Sept. 1858.	Proved useful in keeping the Bazar people in order.
Ditto.........	Meer Kanure Sing, Nephew of the Rajah of Nataghur.	*Englishman*, 15th Sept. 1858.	Succeeded in preventing a band of mutinous Sepoys who had fled from Jullundur from coming into the Hills.

STATEMENTS OF NATIVE FIDELITY EXHIBITED DURING THE MUTINIES OF 1857-58.

Place.	*Person.*	*Authority.*	*Services.*
Sari Sidoo..	Thesildar.	*Delhi Gazette Extra*, quoted for *Englishman*, 20th Sept. 1858.	With police force pursued some 300 Mooltan rebels.
Belliah......	Maha Rajah of.	*Englishman*, 7th Dec. 1858.	Aided with all his means the authorities during the disturbances.
Agra.........	2 Jat Villagers.	*Englishman*, Jan. 1, 1858.	Served and aided an European gentleman and his family in their escape from Delhi.

LIST OF PERSONS REWARDED FOR ACTS OF LOYALTY.

Names.	*Nature of Reward.*
Two Subadars ...	The Title of Bahadur.
Three Sepoys of the Behar Station guards ...	200 Rupees each.
Gomastah of Kootee Etawah ...	Undefined.
Shah Kubbeerooddeen Ahmed and Sujjadeh Nushen of Sasseram ...	Khillut of the value of 10,000 rupees and a Sunnud.
Widow of Syedooddeen, a Kotegusht Darogah ...	Pension.
Chuckdun Sing, Rajah of Seraikillah, in Singbhoom	Khillut.
Seikh Heydayet Ally ...	Rank of Subadar Bahadur and the first class Order of Merit.
Rampergas Sing ...	Present of 1,000 rupees and a commendatory Perwannah.

Names.	*Nature of Reward.*
Hingun Loll, ex.-Tehseeldar ...	Life pension of rupees 100 per mensem, with the honorary title of Deputy Magistrate and Deputy Collector; the pension may be extended to a second life in consideration of his advanced age and impaired constitution.
Seikh Syedooddeen, Kotegusht Darogah of Patna	300 rupees and promotion from the 3rd to the 2nd Grade.
Subadar Major Kassim Ally Khan and Subadar Gunness Doobay ...	First Class of the order of British India with the title of Sirdar Bahadur.
Havildar Futteh Mohamed, 5th Co. ...	Promoted as Jemadar.
Drill Havildar Sheik Ismail, 2d Co. ...	Promoted as Jemadar.
Private (Lance Paick) Sheik Ruheem Buksh, 5th Co. ...	Ditto as Havildar.

Names.	*Nature of Reward.*
Jemadar Cassim Sahib, of the 1st Regiment Infantry, Nagpore Irregular Force ...	Promoted to 3rd Class of the Order of Merit.
Ressaldar Meer Bemda Ally and Woordie Major Meer Burkut Allee ...	Ditto to 3d Class of the Order of British India.
Havildar Pirthee Sing, of the 31st Regiment Native Infantry ...	Rank of Subadar.
Subadars Buctwar Sing, Issuree Buccus Sing, Bhawany Buccus Tewary and Daveedeen ...	Promoted to 3rd Class of the Order of Merit.
Subadar Buctaur Misser, of the 8th Regiment of Infantry, Oude Irregular Force ...	Ditto to 3rd Class of the Order of Merit.
Havildar Khoosial Sing, of the 36th Regiment Native Infantry ...	Ditto to the rank of Subadar.

Names.	*Nature of Reward.*
Subadar Muthora Pursaud, of the 22nd Regiment Bombay Native Infantry ...	Promoted to the 3rd Class of the Order of Merit.
Havildar Sunkehadeen, of the 2nd Infantry, Hyderabad Contingent ...	Ditto to the rank of Subadar.
Naicks Sheik Barry and Sheevapersad of the 2nd Infantry, Hyderabad Contingent ...	Ditto to the rank of Jemadar.
Havildars Sohoi Sing and Cussim Khan, of the 8th Regiment Native Infantry ...	Ditto to the rank of Jemadar.
Ressaldar Munowur Khan, of the 12th Irregular Cavalry. ...	Promoted to First Class of the Order of British India with the title of Bahadur.

Names.	*Nature of Reward.*
Mohamed Buksh Khan, of the 12th Irregular Cavalry. ...	Promoted from the 3rd to the 1st Class of the Order of Merit.
Ressaldar Ismail Khan of the 2nd Cavalry, Hyderabad Contingent. ...	Promoted to rank of Ressaldar Major.
Havildar Adjoodhia Misser, Naick Goojar Khan and Sepoy Dhuttoo Singh. ...	Promoted to the ranks of Subadar, Jemadar and Havildar respectively.
Havildar Gunga Besun, No. 12 Light Field Battery. ...	Promoted as Jemadar.
Two men of the 6th Regiment Native Infantry.	Ditto as Havildar and Naick.
Havildar Muttra Pattuck 21st Regiment Native Infantry. ...	Ditto as Jemadar,
Sepoy Tague Ally Khan, of the 22nd Regiment Native Infantry. ...	Ditto.

Names.	*Nature of Reward*
31st Regt. N. I.—1 Havildar. ...	Promoted as Subadar.
31st Regt. N. I.—11 Naicks. ...	Ditto as Havildar.
31st Regt. N. I.—12 Sepoys. ...	Ditto as Naick.
Two Havildars of the 32nd Regiment Native Infantry. ...	Ditto as Jemadar.
Sepoy Sheik Phultoo of the 34th Regiment Native Infantry. ...	Ditto as Havildar.
Havildar Gungadeen Chowbee of the 35th Regiment Native Infantry.	Ditto as Jemadar.
Havildar Sing Khoosial of the 36th Regiment Native Infantry. ...	Ditto as Subadar.
Two Naicks of the 37th Regiment Native Infantry. ...	Ditto as Havildar.
Twelve Sepoys of the 37th Regiment Native Infantry. ...	Ditto as Naick.
Four Havildars of the 37th Regiment Native Infantry. ...	Ditto as Jemadar.

Names.	*Nature of Reward.*
Sepoy Kehurree Sing of the 63rd Regiment Native Infantry. ...	Promoted as Naick.
Sepoy Sewbuccus Doobey of the 70th Regiment Native Infantry. ...	Ditto as Jemadar.
Naick Oajurh Lullut of the 70th Regiment Native infantry. ...	Ditto as Havildar.
Two Sepoys of the 70th Regiment Native Infantry. ...	Ditto as Naick.
Havildar Bindabun Tewarree of the 73rd Regiment Native Infantry. ...	Ditto as Jamadar.
Nineteen Privates of the Gun Lascar Detail, attached to the 1st Company 3rd Battalion Arty. ...	Promoted to the Third Class of the Order of Merit.
Jemadar Moossum Allee of the 6th Company 9th Battalion Arty. ...	Ditto as Subadar.
Havildar Bhola of ditto ditto. ...	Ditto as Jemadar.

Names.	*Nature of Reward.*
Twenty Privates of ditto ditto. ...	Promoted to the Third Class of the Order of Merit.
Subadar Sheik Golam Ghose of the 4th Punjab Infantry.	Ditto to the Third Class of the Order of Merit.
Subadar Heera Sing of ditto ditto. ...	Ditto to the Second Class of the Order of Merit.
Two Subadars, two Havildars, eight Naicks and twenty Sepoys of the 4th Punjaub Infantry	Promoted to the Third Class of the Order of Merit.
Jemadar Golam Hossein Khan of the 1st Cavalry Hyderabad Contingent.	Ditto to the Third Class of the Order of Merit.
Trooper Rahmut Oollah Khan of ditto ditto. ...	Promoted as Duffadar.
Two Naib Ressaldars Gholam Nubbee Khan and Ahmud Saeed Khan of the 4th Regt. Irregular Cavy. ...	Ditto as Ressaldar.

Names.	*Nature of Reward.*
Duffadar Duraz Khan of the do. do. ...	Promoted as Kote Duffadar.
Nine Sowars of ditto ditto. ...	Ditto as Duffadar.
Subadar Sheikh Khoda Bux of the 56th Regt. Native Infantry. ...	Promoted to the Third Class of the Order of Merit.
Havildar Kesseree Sing of the 1st Light Cavalry.	Promoted as Subadar.
Sepoys Mothoora Pandy and Matubbar Khan of the Ramghur Light Infantry. ...	Ditto as Havildar.
Subadar Major Oomur Khan of the 47th Native Infantry. ...	Promoted to the First Class of the Order of British India with the title of Sirdar Bahadur.
Three Havildars of the 47th Native Infantry.	Ditto as Jamadar.
Naick Daem Khan of the 47th Native Infantry ...	Ditto as Havildar.

Names.	*Nature of Reward.*
Two Sepoys of the 47th Regiment Native Infantry. ...	Promoted to the 3rd Class of the Order of Merit.
Jamadar Mahomed Akrram Khan of the 4th Punjab Cavalry. ...	Promoted as Ressaldar and to the 3rd Class of the Order of Merit.
Sowar Abdoola Khan of do. do. ...	Do. as Duffadar and to the 3rd Class of the Order of Merit.
Ressaldar Allee Woordee Khan and Kote Duffadar Gollam Allee Khan of the 17th Irregular Cavalry, British Troop 1st Brigade Horse Artillery. ...	Promoted to the 3d Class of the Order of Merit.
Jemadar Emam Buksh.	Promoted as Subadar.
Three Havildars ...	Ditto as Jemadar.
Naick Wuzeer Khan. ...	Do. as Havildar and to the 1st Class of the Order of Merit.

Names.	*Nature of Reward.*
Subadar Emam Buksh. ...	Promoted to the 1st Class of the Order of British India with the title of Sirdar Bahadur.
Two Jemadars, ...	Do. to the 2nd Class of the Order of British India with the title of Bahadur.
66 Men, ...	Do. to the 3rd. Class of the Order of Merit.
19 Men, ...	Promotion undefined.
Four men of the 6th Company 9th Battalion Artillery. ...	Promoted to the 3rd Class of the Order of Merit.
Havildar Meer Hyder Ally ...	Promoted as Jemadar.
Three Naicks. ...	Ditto as Havildar.
Fifteen Privates. ...	Ditto as Naick.
Three Lance Naicks of the 1st Company 5th Battalion Arty. ...	Promoted as Havildar and Member of the 3rd Class of the Order of Merit.
Twelve Privates of the same Corps. ...	Promoted as Naick.

Names.	*Nature of Reward.*
Naib Ressaldar Nubbee Buksh Khan, 12th Irregular Cavalry. ...	Ditto as Ressaldar and to the 3rd Class of the Order of Merit.
Four Men, Ditto Ditto.	Ditto as Naib Ressaldar,
Seven men, ditto ditto.	Ditto as Jemadar,
Six Sowars, ditto ditto.	Ditto as Kote Duffadar.
Three Sowars, ditto ditto.	Ditto as Nishanburdar,
Sowar Khas Buksh Khan, ditto ditto. ...	Ditto as Pay Duffadar,
Twenty-three Sowars, ditto ditto. ...	Ditto as Duffadar.
Six Sowars, ditto ditto.	Ditto as Lance Duffadar.
Subadar Mahan Singh, Regiment of Ferozepore.	Ditto as Subadar Major and to the 1st Class Order of Merit,
Jemadar Bhoop Singh, ditto ditto. ...	Ditto as Subadar and to the 1st Class Order of Merit.
Havildars Gohon Shah and Heera Sing, ditto ditto. ...	Ditto to the 2nd Class Order of Merit.

Names.	*Nature of Reward.*
Jemadar Secundar Khan, ditto ditto. ...	Promoted as Subadar.
Sixteen Havildars, ditto ditto. ...	Ditto as Jemadar,
Sixteen Naicks, ditto ditto. ...	Ditto as Havildar.
Two hundred and sixty-eight Sepoys, ditto ditto. ...	Ditto as Naick.
Jemadar Peer Buccus Khan, 1st Regiment Oude Local Infantry. ...	Ditto as Subadar and to the 2nd Class Order of Merit.
Havildar Putram Misser, ditto ditto. ...	Ditto as Jemadar.
Five Sepoys ditto ditto.	Ditto as Havildar.
Sewdenee Misser, ditto ditto. ...	Ditto as Naick.
Subadar Seosahæ Sing of the 40th Regt. Native Infantry. ...	Promoted to the 2nd Class of the Order of British India with the title of Bahadur.
Havildar Naick Singh 40th Native Infantry. ...	Promoted as Jemadar.

Names.	*Nature of Reward.*
Havildar Issurrie Sing, ditto ditto....	Promoted as Subadar
" Sooroojbullee Ram ditto ditto. ...	Ditto as Jemadar
Ramphool Singh, ditto ditto. ...	Ditto ditto.
Three Naicks, ditto ditto.	Ditto as Havildar.
Three Sepoys, ditto ditto.	Ditto as Naick.
Subadar Major Deen Mohamed 2nd Company 8th Battalion Artillery. ...	Ditto to the 1st Class Order of Merit.
Subadar Rampersaud, ditto ditto. ...	Ditto ditto.
Two men, ditto ditto...	Promoted as Jemadar.
Two men, ditto ditto. ...	Ditto as Jemadar and to the 3rd Class Order of Merit.
Five men, ditto ditto. ...	Ditto as Havildar.
Thirteen men, ditto ditto...	Ditto as Naick
Two Sirdars of D. Company Ordnance Drivers, attached to No. 2 Light Field Battery. ...	Ditto to the 2nd Class Order of merit.

Names.	*Nature of Reward.*
Twelve men of the same Corps. ...	Promoted as Sirdar.
Khan Sing of No. 1 H. Light Fleld Battery. ...	Ditto as Jemadar and 2nd Class Order of Merit.
Two men of No. 2 Light Field Battery. ...	Ditto as Subadar and do. do.
Seven men of the same corps. ...	Ditto as Jemadar.
Two men of H. Light Field Battery. ...	Ditto as Havildar.
Five men of Drivers, attached to No. 2 Battery. ...	Ditto as Sirdar.
Two men of No. 3, H. Light Field Battery. ...	Ditto as Subabar and 1st Class Order of Merit.
Doyal Singh of the same Corps. ...	Ditto as Jamadar.
Three men of ditto. ...	Ditto as Havildar.
Two men of Drivers No. 3, Battery. ...	Ditto as Sirdar.
Subadar Khalsa Sing of the Reserve Company of Artillery. ...	Promoted to the 3rd Class Order of Merit.

Names.	*Nature of Reward.*
Sepoy Kullian Sing of the 42nd Native Light Infantry. ...	Restored to the service without forfeiture of pay and promoted to the rank of Naick.
Jemadar Oodaraj Sookul of the 74th Native Infantry. ...	Promoted to the Rank of Subadar and 2nd Class of the Order of British India.
Subadar Nehal Sing of the Bengal Police Battalion. ...	Ditto to the 1st Class of the Order of Merit.
Trooper Ullee Mahomed of the 5th Troop 1st Brigade Horse Arty. ...	Ditto to the 3rd Class of the Order of Merit.
Ressaldar Boolund Khan of the 8th Regiment Irregular Cavalry. ...	Ditto to the 1st Class of the Order of British India, with the title of Sirdar Bahadoor.

Names.	*Nature of Reward.*
Ressaldar Hoossain Ali Khan, of the 17th Irregular Cavalry. ...	Promoted to the 2nd Class of the Order of British India, with the title of Bahadoor.
Three Subadars of the Sylhet Light Infantry Battalion. ...	Ditto to the 2nd Class of the Order of British India, with the title of Bahadoor.
Naick Oree Misser of the late 7th Infantry Gwalior C'ntingent. ...	Promoted as Havildar.
Four men of the same Corps. ...	Ditto as Naick.
Sowar Mohamed Zuman Khan of the 1st Punjaub Cavalry. ...	Ditto to the Rank of Duffadar.
Subadar Doolaram of the 2nd Assam Light Infantry. ...	Promoted to the 2nd Class of the Order of British India, with the title of Bahadoor.

Names.	*Nature of Reward.*
Rajah Jyperkash Singh of Deo, in the Zillah of Behar. ...	Title of Maharajah with a suitable Khelat.
Private Dyal Sing and Jemadar Heerah Sing of No. 3, Horse Battery, Oude Irregular Force. ...	Promoted as Havildar and Subadar respectively.
Havildar Shaik Mokhum of the 50th Native Infantry. ...	Ditto as Jemadar,
Two Naicks of the same Corps. ...	Ditto as Havildar,
Eleven Sepoys of the same Corps. ...	Ditto as Naick.
Jemadar Muhasee Lall of the Kotah Contingent, Infantry. ...	Ditto as Subadar.
Duffadar Sheikh Ruheem Oolah of the Kotah Contingent, Cavalry. ...	Ditto as Naib Ressaldar.
Four Duffadars of the same Corps. ...	Ditto as Jemadar.
Five Sowars of the same Corps. ...	Promoted as Duffadar.

Names.	*Nature of Reward.*
Subadar Rugbeer Sing, Infantry Ressaldar Dulail Khan Woordie Major, ...	Ditto to the 1st Class of the order of British India with the title of Sirdar Bahadoor.
Two Duffadars of the Jaudpore Legion. ...	Ditto as Jemadar and 3rd Class of the Order of Merit.
Three Subadars of the Simoor Battalion. ...	Ditto to the 2nd Class of the Order of British India, with the title of Bahadoor.
Jemadar Buddul Tapah of do. do. ...	Ditto to 2nd Class of the Order of Merit.
Twenty men of ditto ditto. ...	Ditto to the 3rd Class of the Order of Merit.
Ressaldar Ameer Ally Khan of the Behar Irregular Horse. ...	Ditto to the 2nd Class of the Order of British India with the title of Bahadoor.

Names.	*Nature of Reward.*
Subadar Unjore Tewary of the 1st Regiment Native Infantry. ...	Ditto to the 1st Class of the Order of British India, with the title of Sirdar Bahadoor.
Three men of the Southern Mahratta Irregular Horse. ...	Promoted to the 3rd Class of the Order of Merit.
Havildar Mothura Pandy of the Ramghur Light Infantry Battalion. ...	Ditto to the 3rd Class of the Order of Merit.
Ressaldar Mir Umjid Ali of the 2nd Regiment of Cavalry Scindhia's Contingent. ...	Promoted to the 1st Class of the Order of Merit.
Duffadar Mir Koorshiad Ali of the same Corps.	Ditto as Jemadar and 2nd Class of the Order of Merit.
Seven Sowars of the same Corps. ...	Ditto as Duffadar and 3rd Class of the Order of Merit.

Names.	*Nature of Reward.*
Nineteen men of the same Corps.	... Promoted to the 3rd Class of the Order of Merit.
Three men of the 6th Irregular Cavalry.	... Ditto to the 3rd Class of the Order of Merit.
Havildar Major Kunjul Sing of the 25th Bombay Native Infantry.	Ditto as Jemadar and 3rd Class of the Order of Merit.
N ique Doorga Tewaree of the same Corps.	... Ditto as Havildar and 3rd Class of the Order of Merit.
Private Punnoo Loll of the same Corps.	... Ditto as Naique and 3rd Class of the Order of Merit.
Subadar Major Jowahire Tewaree of the 43rd Native Infantry.	... Ditto to the 2nd Class of the Order of British India with the title of Bahadur.

Names.	*Nature of Reward.*
Havildar Dilkurn Thapa of the Artillery Company attached to the 2nd Assam Light Infantry. ...	Promoted as Jemadar.
Havildar Thelookdarrie, Syce Driver of the U. Company. ...	Ditto as Jemadar.
Two Gun Lascars of the 2nd Troop 1st Brigade Horse Artillery. ...	Ditto as Jemadar.
Three Gun Lascars of the 2nd Troop 1st Brigade Horse Artillery. ...	Ditto as Naick.
Jemadar Sadhoo Sing, and Duffadar Jewan Sing, of the 1st Cavalry, Hyderabad Contingent....	Ditto to the 2nd Class of the Order of Merit.
Trooper Koodrut Ally Khan, do. do. ...	Ditto as Duffadar and 3rd Class of the Order of Merit.
Trooper Shah Meer Khan, and Trooper Shah Noor Khan, do. do. ...	Ditto as Duffadar.
Two Havildars the 3rd Infantry Hyderabad Contingent. ...	Ditto as Jemadar.

Names.	*Nature of Reward.*
Two Privates ditto ditto.	Ditto as Havildar.
Ressaldar Abdool Raimen Khan of the 1st Cavalry Hyderabad Contingent.	Promoted to the 2nd Class of the Order of British India with the title of Bahadur.
Two Ressaldars of the 3rd Seikh Cavalry. ...	Ditto to the 2nd Class of the Order of British India with the title of Bahadur.
Six men of the same Corps. ...	Ditto to the 3rd Class of the Order of Merit.
Jemadar Durion of the late 4th Native Infantry.	Ditto as Subadar and 3rd Class of the Order of Merit.
Ressaldar Jowaher Sing of the 1st Seikh Cavalry.	Ditto to the 1st Class of the Order of British India with the title of Sirdar Bahadur.
Naib Ressaldar Unnoop Sing of ditto ditto ...	Ditto to the 3rd Class of the Order of Merit.
Havildar Utter Sing of the Regiment of Loodianah. ...	Promoted as Jemadar.

Names.	*Nature of Reward.*
Havildar Chur Sing of the Regiment of Loodianah. ...	Ditto as Subadar.
Six Havildars of the Regiment of Loodianah.	Ditto as Jemadar.
Five Naicks of the Regiment of Loodianah. ...	Ditto as Havildar.
Thirty-six Sepoys of the Regiment of Loodianah.	Ditto as Naicks.
Duffadar Secunder Ally Khan of the 3rd Regiment Irregular Cavalry.	Ditto as Jemadar.
Four men of the 13th Regiment Irregular Cavalry. ...	Ditto as Jemadar.
Kote Duffadar Delaur Hossein of the 13th Regiment Irregular Cavalry. ...	Ditto as Ressaldar.
Three Duffadars of the 13th Regiment Irregular Cavalry. ...	Ditto as Jemadar.
Thirty-three Sowars of the 13th Regiment Irregular Cavalry. ...	Ditto as Duffadar.
Two Duffadars of the 1st Cavalry Hyderabad Contingent. ...	Ditto as Jemadar

Names.	*Nature of Reward.*
Two Havildars of the 1st Infantry Nagpore Irregular Force. ...	Promoted as Jemadar.
Two Naicks of the Nepaul Residency Escort.	Ditto as Havildar.
Three men of the Nagpore Irregular Cavalry.	Ditto as Jemadar.
Havildar Boolakie Khan of the Ramgurh Battalion. ...	Ditto as Jemadar.
Sepoy Doorgah Misser of the 8th Regiment Oude Infantry. ...	Ditto as Naick.
Duffadar Kurrum Shair K an of the 5th Regt. Irregular Cavalry. ...	Ditto as Jemadar.
Three Sowars of the 5th Regiment Irregular Cavalry. ...	Ditto as Duffadar.
Two Naicks of the 2nd Infantry Hyderabad Contingent. ...	Ditto as Jemadar.
Havildar Sirdar Khan of the 4th Company 9th Bengal Artillery. ...	Ditto as Subadar.
Private Seetaram of the 4th Co. 9th Bengal Artillery. ...	Ditto as Havildar.

Names.	*Nature of Reward.*
Two Havildars of the 8th Regt. Native Infantry. ...	Promoted as Jemadars.
Four Sowars of the 2nd Irregular Cavalry. ...	Ditto to the 3rd Class of the Order of Merit.
Sepoy Gobin Sing of the 56th Regt. Native Infantry. ...	Ditto as Jemadar.
Subadar Meer Jaffer of the 1st Punjaub Infantry.	Ditto to the 2nd Class of the Order of Merit.
Havildar Shajadah of the 1st Punjaub Infantry.	Ditto to the 3rd Class of the Order of Merit.
Naick Sheer Ali of the 2nd Punjaub Infantry. ...	Ditto to the 3rd Class of the Order of Merit.
Two Sepoys of the 2nd Punjaub Infantry. ...	Ditto to the 3rd Class of the Order of Merit.
Four Sepoys of the 4th Punjaub Infantry. ...	Ditto to the 3rd Class of the Order of Merit.
Subadar Doolar Tewarry of the 12th Regt. Native Infantry. ...	Ditto to the 1st Class of the Order of British India with the title of Sirdar Bahadur.

Names.	*Nature of Reward.*
Subadar Sheick Heydayet Ali of the Bengal Police Battalion. ...	Promoted to the 1st Class of the Order of British India with the title of Sirdar Bahadur and the rank of Sub-Lieut.
Subadar Sheodeen Singh of the 9th Regt. Native Infantry. ...	Ditto to the 2nd Class of the Order of British India with the title of Bahadur.
S badar Major Meer Ameer Ally of the 32nd Regiment N. I. ...	Ditto to the 2nd Class of the Order of British India with the title of Bahadur.
Four Subadars of the 11th Regt. Native Infantry. ...	Ditto as Subadar Major.
Eleven Havildars, ditto ditto. ...	Ditto as Jemadar.
Eight Naicks, ditto ditto.	Ditto as Havildar.
Sixty-nine Sepoys, ditto ditto. ...	Ditto as Naick.

Names.	*Nature of Reward.*
Two Subadars and one Jemadar of the 11th Regiment Native Infantry.	Promoted to the 2nd Class of the Order of British India with the title of Bahadur.
Two Naicks of the 11th Regiment Native Infantry. ...	Ditto to the 3rd Class of the Order of Merit.
Subadar Gunga Sing of the 2nd Grenadier Regiment Bombay Native Infantry. ...	Ditto to the 1st Class of the Order of Britsh India with the title of Sirdar Bahadur.
Ressaldar Jye Sing of the 1st Regt, Punjaub Cavalry. ...	Ditto to the 1st Class of the Order of British India with the title of Sirdar Bahadur.
Jemadar Suffer Ali Beg.	Ditto as Ressaldar.
Duffadar Kullian Singh.	Ditto as Jemadar.
Duffadars Abas Ali Beg.	Ditto as Jemadar.
Trooper Rohomon Beg and Trooper Golam Abas. ...	Ditto as Duffadar.

Names.	*Nature of Reward.*
Major Captain Shree Bhukut Khauka, Commanding the Ramdul Regt., Captain Dercidass Opadiah of the same corps, Capt. Kooloopurshad Sing Bushnial, Commanding the Goorkha Regt. ...	Thanked by the Governor-General.
Maharajah Jung Bahadur, Brigadier Junga Dage, Colonel Lall Singh and Capt. Sugan Singh and the other Goorka Officers. ...	Thanked by the Governor-Genl.
Subadar Major Mehtab Khan, of the rural Police, and Ressaldar Ali Mahomed of the mounted Police of Sikrampore. ...	Promoted to the 3rd Class of the Order of Merit.
Jemadar Narain Singh of the Regiment of Ludhianah. ...	Ditto as Subadar.

Names.	*Nature of Reward*
Abdoolrazack Khan, Trooper 1st Troop 4th Cavalry. ...	Promoted to the Order of Merit as Jemadar.
Gya Dutt Sing Tewarree, Sepoy of the 67th Regt. Native Infantry. ...	Ditto as Havildar, Order of Merit.
Subadar Gokul Sing of the 4th Punjaub Infantry. ...	Ditto to the 2nd Class of the Order of British India, with the title of Bahadur.
Lieut.-Colonel Indra Sing, Commanding the Napalese Troops. ...	Thanked by the President in Council.
Jemadar Hurnauth Sing of the Ramghur Light Infantry Battalion. ...	Promoted to the 3rd Class of the Order of Merit.
Subadar Meer Jaffar of the 1st Punjab Infantry.	Ditto to the 1st Class of the Order of British India, with the title of Sirdar Bahadur,

Names.	*Nature of Reward.*
Havildars Omed Khan, Hoonumaun Sing, Bugle Major and Emambuccus.	Promoted as Jemadar.
Colonel Shum Shere Sing and the Troops under his command. ...	Thanked by the Government of India.
Havildar Punchum Sing, and Naick Punch Cowriz, of the 20th Regiment Native Infantry. ...	Promoted as Jemadar.
1st Company Subadar Major Ummul Ali Shah, 2nd Company Subadar Major Jugroop Sing and Subadar Nehal Singh. ...	Promoted to the 2nd Class of the Order of British India with the title of Bahadur.
1st Co. Jemadar Dhull Singh and Jemadar Matah Singh. ...	Ditto to the 3rd Class of the Order of Merit.
Havildars Wuryam Singh and Emam Shah of the 1st Comy., and Havildars Rae Singh and Futteh Khan. ...	Ditto as Jemadar.

Names.	*Nature of Reward.*
Naick Gear Sing and Sepoy Jean Singh, 2nd Co. ...	Promoted as Havildar.
Sepoy Seccundur Khan, Sepoy Gourmookh Sing and Eseree. ...	Ditto as Naick.
Jemadar Kunnie Sing of the Punjaub Infantry. ...	Ditto as Subadar.
Havildar Peer Khan. ...	Ditto as Jemadar.
Sepoys Ramdyal Singh, Thakoor Singh and Doorga Singh. ...	Ditto as Havildar.
Subadar Sew Lal of the Artillery of the Bhoopal Contingent. ...	Ditto to the 3rd Class of the order of Merit.
Havildar Moonalaul Pundy of the Bhoopal Contingent. ...	Ditto as Jemadar.
Havildar Ramloll Misser.	Ditto ditto.
Naicks Bhowany Deen and Mahomed Yar Khan.	Ditto as Havildar.
Thirteen Gunners of the same corps. ...	Ditto to the post of Naick.
Subadar Hubeeb Khan of the 1st Punjaub Cavalry. ...	Ditto to the 2nd Class of the Order of British India.

Names.	*Nature of Reward.*
Two Subadars, three Jemadars, six Sepoys, three Havildars and thirteen Naicks of the 1st Punjaub Cavalry. ...	Promoted to the 3rd Class of the Order of Merit.
Jemadar Lochun Pandee of the 11th Regt. Native Infantry. ...	Ditto to the 2nd Class of the Order of British India with the title of Bahadur.
Three Naicks of the 11th Regiment Native Infantry. ...	Ditto to the 3rd Class of the Order of Merit.
Jemadar Dunnyee of the Gun Lascar Detail attached to the 1st Company 3rd Brattalion Arty. ...	Ditto as Subadar.
Havildar Culloo of ditto. ...	Ditto as Jemadar.
Private Sheick Madar Bux of ditto. ...	Ditto as Naick.
Two men of the Lucknow Magazine. ...	Ditto as Jemadar.

Names.	*Nature of Reward.*
Two men of the 4th Company 1st Battalion Artillery. ...	Promoted as Jemadar.
Two men of the same Corps. ...	Ditto as Havildar.
Two men of the P. Company Syce Drivers. ...	Ditto as Naick.
Five men of the same Corps. ...	Ditto as Havildar.
Subadar Major Ummer Sing, 13th Native Infantry. ...	Promoted to the 1st Class Order of Merit.
Ten Subadars, ditto ditto. ...	Ditto to the 2nd Class Order of Merit.
Three Havildars, ditto ditto. ...	Ditto as Jemadars and 3rd Class Order of Merit.
Fourteen Havildars, 13th N. I. ...	Ditto as Jemadar.
Twenty-three Naicks, ditto ditto. ...	Ditto as Havildar.
Fity-five Sepoys, ditto ditto. ...	Ditto as Naick.
Nineteen men, ditto ditto. ...	3 month's pay.

Names.	*Nature of Reward.*
Subadar Sewraj Sing, the new Cawnpore Cavalry, ...	Promoted to the 3rd Class Order of Merit.
Three Naicks, ditto ditto. ...	Ditto as Havildar.
Three Sepoys, ditto ditto. ...	Ditto as Naick.
Subadar Major and Bahadur Madheý Khan, 7th Light Cavalry. ...	Promoted to the 1st Class Order of Merit.
Two Subadars, ditto ditto. ...	Ditto to the 2d Class Order of Merit.
Shaick Emam Bux, ditto ditto. ...	Ditto to the 1st Class Native Doctor and 500 Rs.
Seven men, ditto ditto. ...	Undefined.
Ten men, 41st Regt. Native Infantry. ...	Undefined.
Gyand Sing, 48th N. Infantry. ...	Promoted as Sirdar Bahadur and 1st Class Order of Merit.

Names.	*Nature of Reward.*
Seven men, ditto ditto. ...	Promoted as Subadar Bahadur and 2nd Class Order of Merit.
Herah loll Misser, ditto ditto. ...	Ditto as Subadar.
Twelve men, ditto ditto. ...	Ditto as Jemadar.
Eighteen Naicks, ditto ditto. ...	Ditto as Havildar.
Two men, ditto ditto, ...	108 Rupees.
Rambuccus, ditto ditto. ...	78 Rupees.
Four men, ditto ditto. ...	66 Rupees.
Five men, ditto ditto. ...	30 Rupees.
Subadar Sew Sing, 71st N. I. ...	Promoted to the 1st Class Order of Merit.
Four men, 71st N. Infantry. ...	Ditto as Subadar and 2nd Class Order of Merit.
Fourteen Havildars, ditto ditto. ...	Ditto as Jemadar.
Jemadar Ramchurrun, do. do. ...	Ditto to the 3rd Class Order of Merit.
Twenty-one Naicks ditto ditto. ...	Ditto as Havildar.
Drum Major Edward Hughes, ditto ditto. ...	68 Rupees.

Names.	*Nature of Reward.*
Subadar Jungah Sing, 1st Regt. Irregular Infantry. ...	Promoted as Sirdar Bahadur, and 1st Class Order of Merit.
Jemadar Mokhun Sing, do. do. ...	Ditto as Subadar.
Havildar Sunnath Pandee. do. do. ...	Ditto as Jemadar Bahadur, and 2nd Class Order of Merit.
Two Havildars, ditto ditto. ...	Ditto as Jemadar.
Three Sepoys, do. do. ...	Ditto as Naick.
Sepoy Khoolyer Doobey, Local Infantry. ...	Promoted as Havildar.
Sepoy Poorun Doobey. ...	Ditto as Naick.
Five Sepoys. ...	Undefined.
Naib Ressaldar Shere Sing of the 1st Oude Irregular Cavalry. ...	Promoted as Ressaldar and the 2nd Class of the Order of British India with the title of Bahadur.
Subadar Runbeer Sing of the Nusseree Battalion. ...	Ditto to the 3rd Class of the Order of Merit.

Names.	*Nature of Reward*
Ressaldar Major Mahomed Oomur Khan of the 4th Cavalry Hyderabad Contingent. ...	Promoted to the 1st Class of the Order of British India with the title of Sirdar Bahadur,
Two men, 71st N. I. ...	24 Rupees,
Three men, ditto ditto. ...	18 Rupees.
Ressaldar Seetul Sing of the late 3rd Oude Irregular Cavalry. ...	Promoted to the Ressaldar and the 1st Class of the Order of Merit.
Lehna Sing, Seikh, Zemindar of Thannessur.	Ditto to the rank and position of Jemadar in the 8th Regiment Irregular Cavalry.
Ressaldar Soobhan Khan of the 3rd Irregular Cavalry. ...	Ditto to the 2nd Class of the Order of Merit.
Subadar Devey Deen of the 31st Native Infantry. ...	Ditto to the 2nd Class of the Order of Merit.

Names.	*Nature of Reward.*
Subadar Pertee Sing of the 31st Native Infantry.	Promoted to the 3rd Class of the Order of Merit.
Three Subadars, two Jemadars, eleven Havildars, four Naicks, and thirty-six Sepoys of the 31st Regiment N. I. ...	Ditto to the 3rd Class of the Order of Merit.
Jemadar Mahomed Khan of the 6th Regiment Light Cavalry. ...	Ditto as Subadar.
Jemadar Sundial Sing of the Bengal Police Battalion, 31st N. I. transferred to Light Infantry Regiment. ...	Ditto to the 3rd Class of the Order of Merit.
Bhooray Sing of Bettara. ...	500 Rupees and proprietary right in a village paying an annual revenue of 1,000 Rs.
Sheo Gholam Sing & Aurjoo Sing. ...	1,000 Rupees.

Names.	*Nature of Reward.*
Luchee Kahar of Tilla, Boodhoo Sais, Jodhun Sais, and Moosa Dhobey.	100 Rupees each.
Two Jemadars and seven Havildars of the 3rd Light Cavalry. ...	Promoted as Subadar
Naick Rugnauth Sing of ditto. ...	Ditto as Jemadar.
Thirteen Troopers of Ditto. ...	Ditto as Havildar.
Subadar Ram Churn Sing of ditto. ...	Ditto to the 2nd Class Order of Merit.
Two Subadars of ditto. ...	Ditto to the 3rd Class Order of Merit.
Two Sepoys of the 1st Irregular Infantry. ...	Ditto as Havildar.
Subadars Bindadeen Tewaree and Achaiba Lolla of the 73rd Regt. Native Infantry. ...	Ditto to the 1st Class of the Order of Merit.
Havildar Shaik Khoaj-bux and Naick Ramjun Khan of the 8th Regt. N. I. ...	Ditto to the Rank of Subadar and Jemadar respectively.

Names.	*Nature of Reward.*
Havildar Thackour Sing of the Bengal Sheikh Police Battalion. ...	Promoted as Jemadar and 200 Rs.
Syud Kheir Shah, Kardar of Jacobabad in Upper Sinde. ...	Title of Khan Bahadur.
Naick Sewdeen Doobe of the 63rd Regt. N. I. ...	Promoted to the Rank of Jemadar.
Havildar Mehurban Tewarree of the Bengal Police Battalion. ...	Ditto to the 2nd Class of the Order of Merit
Jemadar Sewdial Sing of the same Corps. ...	Ditto ditto.
Five men of the same Corps. ...	Ditto to the 3rd Class of the Order of Merit.
Ressaldar Mirza Ahmed Beg of Hodson's Horse. ...	Ditto to the Rank of Ressaldar.
Subadar Banee Sing of the 1st Company Hyderabad Contingent. ...	Ditto to the 2nd Class of the Order of British India with the title of Bahadur.

Names.	*Nature of Reward.*
Havildar Major Syed Meeun of the same Corps. ...	Promoted as Jemadar.
Subadar Major Tucketram of the 4th Company Hyderabad Contingent. ...	Promoted to the 2nd Class of the Order of British India with the title of Bahadur.
Acting Havildar Major Tacoor Persaud of the same Corps. ...	Promoted as Jemadar.
Ressaldar Major Mirza Zoolficar. ...	Promoted to the 2nd Class of the Order of British India.
Ali Beg of the 1st Cavalry Hyderabad Contingent. ...	With the title of Bahadur.
Duffadar Kullundur Beg of the same Corps. ...	Promoted as Jemadar and Member of the 3rd Class of the Order of Merit.
Two Duffadars of the same Corps. ...	Ditto as Jemadar.

Names.		*Nature of Reward.*
Trooper Syed Russool of the same Corps.	...	Promoted as Duffadar.
Bargheer Syud Shureef of the 2nd Cavalry Hyderabad Contingent.	...	Promoted as Duffadar and to the 3rd Class of the Order of Merit.
Ressaldars Fazil Khan and Deedar Bux Khan of the 4th Cavalry, Hd. Qrt.	...	Promoted to the 3rd Class of the Order of Merit.
Trumpeter Futeh Khan of the same Corps.	...	Promoted as Trumpet Major.
Havildar Tilluck Pandy of the Regiment of Lucknow.	...	Promoted to the 3rd Class of the Order of Merit.
Subadar Shaik Ibrahim of the 19th Regt. Madras Native Infantry.	...	Ditto ditto.
Two men of the Keman Battalion.	...	Ditto ditto.

Names.	*Nature of Reward.*
Naick Shaik Loll Mahomed of the 6th Company 9th Battalion Arty.	Promoted as Havildar and to the 3rd Class of the Order of Merit.
Woordie Major Meer Burkulelly of the 1st Regiment Irregular Cavalry. ...	Promoted as Ressaldar and to the 1st Class of the Order of British India with the title of Sirdar Bahadur.
Three Ressaldars and two Naib Ressaldars of the same Corps. ...	Promoted to the 2nd Class of the Order of British India with the title of Bahadur.
Two men of the same Corps. ...	Ditto to the 2nd Class of the Order of Merit.
Four Duffadars of the Joudpore Legion. ...	Promoted as Jemadar.
Ressaldar Mahomed Wuzir Khan of the Bengal Police Battalion.	Ditto to the 2nd Class of the Order of British India with the title of Bahadur.

Names.	*Nature of Reward.*
Ressaldar Meer Mahomed Ali of the Guzerat Irregular Horse. ...	Promoted to the 3rd Class of the Order of Merit.
Naib Ressaldar Meer Sbamsad Allee of the Guzerat Irregular Horse.	Ditto to the 3rd Class of the Order of Merit.
2 Jat Villagers of Agra....	100 Rs. each.
Thakoor Govind Sing of Allyghur. ...	A palankeen carriage and a pair of horses.
The Native Establishment and the Nizam Guard of the Opium Factory of Allygunge....	Six months' salary.
Subadar Gobind. ...	1,000 Rupees.
Salamut Roy, Deputy Collector of Allyghur....	Khelat of thousand Rupees.
Gungaram Misser and Chundun Persad of Bajheyara. ...	The proprietary right of a confiscated village or villages assessed at 2,600 Rupees per annum, and for their lives the remission of $\frac{1}{4}$ to the assessed revenue.

Names.	*Nature of Reward.*
Bhoorary Singh of Bettara, Shahjehanpore.	The proprietary right of a village or villages assessed at 1,000 Rupees per annum and for his life the remission of ¼ the assessed value.
Bhobaney Sing of Moneypore. ...	Title of Rajah, a Khelat and the confiscated estate of Jye Singh.
Setaram Misser of Bangeon. ...	The proprietary right of a village assessed at 2,00 Rupees per annum with the above remission.
Bhorary Singh. ...	Compensation for the losses suffered by him
Sheogolam Singh and Harjo Singh. ...	1,000 Rupees each.
Luchee Kahar of Tilla, Bhoodo Sais, Jodhan Sais and Mosho Dhobey. ...	100 Rupees each.

Names.		*Nature of Reward.*
The Rajah of Bansee,	...	Khelat of Rupees 5,000 and a portion of the confiscated estates of the rebel Rajah of Nuggur,
Nawab Jahn Firh Khan Bahadur of Sirdhina.	...	Pension of 1,000 Rupees to be perpetuated to the lineal male heirs and a perpetuity in confiscated villages assessed at Rupees 1,000 with certain conditions.
Rajah of Berkewer,	...	Most cordial thanks of the Governor General and a Jagheer of more than one lakh of Rupees.
Ramchunder Baboo,	...	Khelat of five pieces and Co.'s Rupees 2,000.
Rampersaud Zemindar of Bosselle.	...	A handsome present.
Meer Bahad Sing.	...	Title of Rajah.
Ramperkas Sing.	...	1,000 Rupees.

Names.	*Nature of Reward.*
Ramnarain Sing of Agra.	... Received pardon for his son Bhagoo Sing who was sentenced to transportation for life in 1834 for affray.
Rajah of Gorruckpore.	... Appellation of Nizam of Gorruckpore.
Two Mahomedan Zemindars.	... A Gold Watch and chains each.
A Hindu Darogah.	... A splendid sword.
Some Sheiks.	... Medals.
Parties who protected Captain Gowan in Rohilkhund.	... Confiscated estate of a certain rebel chief.
Golab Khan, a rebel spy.	... Handsome presents.
Sepoys who rendered good services to Lieut. Owen on his route from Jounpore.	... Handsome rewards and sununds.
Rajah of Nabath.	... A Jagheer of Rs. 1,15,000 per annum.
Rajah of Sismoor.	... A Khelat of 5,000 Rupees.

Names.	*Nature of Reward.*
Keonthul Rannak.	... Sunund of Rajah and a present.
Takhoor of Khota.	... Sunund of Rajah and a Khelat of 1,000 Rupees.
Rannahs of Bhoogol and Joobul.	... Thousand Rupees each.
Rannah of Dhamee.	... A moiety of his tribute remitted to him for his lifetime.
Jye Sing.	... A Khelat of 600 Rupees.
Kooer Luchmon Singh.	... Promoted to the 2nd grade Deputy Collector of Etwah and received a Khelat of 2,000 Rupees.
Rajah Gudeladhur Narain Sing of Keeonghur.	... Received personal thanks from the Governor-General.
Rajah Teekhun Sing of Allyghur.	... Certain valuable lands
Mahomed Ali and family.	... A certain Zemindary.
Havildar Nursea and Jemadars Bhagootoo and Nutherana of the Police Zemindary.	... Silver Bangles, &c.

Names.	*Nature of Reward.*
Four Artillery men who accompanied Capt. Bouggs in his expedition against Meuloung.	A handsome donation.
Certain women of Allahabad for rescuing a European girl. ...	Undefined.
A Mahomedan who protected Mrs. Jervis. ...	Ditto.
Lalla Joteepersad. ...	Valuable Jagheer lands.
Baboo Pearymohun Banarjea, *alias* the "fighting Moonsiff." ...	Some Jagheer lands.
A Mahomedan of Delhi.	Some handsome rewards for saving the lives of fifty European fugitives.

Numerous other persons have also received handsome rewards whose names we have not seen published, or if published have not met our eyes. Several Rajahs and Chiefs are, it is said, coming from Upper India to receive Khelats and other honors on account of the eminent services rendered by them during the mutinies. We think the moral effect of these rewards will be great if the Government publish a list of the persons thus rewarded, and cause them to be proclaimed throughout the length and breadth of the country. When Scinde was conquered Lord Ellenborough ordered a Convention of the Chiefs and Sirdars commanding them to thus meet togather to pay *salaams* to the Sircar Bahadoor before its then Governor Sir Charles Napier. If in the same manner, an assembly of the loyal Chiefs, Rajahs and Sirdars had been called on the day of the Queen's Proclamation to receive in the gracious presence of the Noble Viceroy and Suite, the rewards which their distinguished services have so eminently deserved, the proceeding would not only have added to the *eclat* of that most momentous occasion, but would have also had the advantage of so installing the affection and esteem of the people for Her Majesty's direct rule thus assumes as to last, which any one acquainted with Asiatic feelings will readily understand, for centuries to come. The opportunity however is not entirely past, [and we hope something will be made of the rumoured durbar of the Rajahs and Chiefs to be rewarded. The true statesmanship for Europeans in Asia consists in the adaptation of European ideas of civilization and progress to Asiatic notions of society and government and in the working of them together as a harmonious whole, and in all public measures it is of the highest importance for our rulers to bear this truth in mind.

We are sorry to observe that persons whose antecedents and known habits of thought give them claim to public attention, still acquiesce in the senseless cry raised at the height of the panic days, by a portion of the Calcutta Europeans, better known as the Leaguers, viz., that the quiet people of Bengal were the enemies of Government, and that whatever loyalty they expressed or evinced was confined to words and never wooed action. Mr. Bruce Norton, we are mortified to find, echoes the same cry. His knowledge of Indian matters, the just and generous spirit with which he used to treat of Indian subjects in the columns of the *Madras Athæneum* and his accurate appreciation of the native races, their feelings and virtues, indicated in his previous writings on India, fairly led us to hope for justice to the Indians at his hands, especially now when the mists which hitherto shrouded Indian questions, have been cleared away by the light of the Sepoy revolution. But we have been disappointed. Mr. Norton, in his recent work entitled, "Topics for Indian Statesmen" takes a

THE SECRETARY TO THE GOVERNMENT OF BENGAL TO THE MAGISTRATE OF HOOGHLY.

Fort William, June 22nd, 1857.

SIR,

I am directed to acknowledge the receipt of your letter of the 20th instant, giving cover to a memorial from certain inhabitants of Ooterpara and other adjacent villages, wherein they express much apprehension, in consequence of the desertions from the ranks of the disarmed Sepoys at Barrackpore, and recommending the entertainment of an additional Police force, consisting of 600 men, of the Agooree and Gowala classes, for the maintenance of order in your district in the event of any disturbance arising.

2. In reply, I am desired to observe that, under Act 17 of 1857, you are employed to arrest the deserters, the number of whom, however, appears to be greatly exaggerated by public apprehension.

3. Under the circumstances represented by you, the Lieutenant-Governor authorizes, as an experimental measure, the organization of a central Police force at the Sudder Station of Hooghly, consisting of people of the classes described in your letter; and should the experiment prove successful, His Honor will be prepared

'They have shared in no peril, they have 'volunteered no services, they have not lent us 'their cattle without an Impressment Act, and 'expressions of loyalty, after the fall of Delhi, 'may be as good policy as they are racy of 'expression. But the truth is, that these memo-'rials and addresses are the merest sham conceiv-'able." We believe all memorials and addresses, whether European or Native, to be very often the purest shams possible, but as regards the loyalty of the Bengalees, we have no hesitation in that Mr. Norton is entirely wrong: they did come forward with their cattle, and if they had not we should not have been able to have procured one single hackery in spite of fifty Impressment Acts. If Mr. Norton were to go into a Bengalee village armed with an Impressment Act, he might find a few broken wheels and a halt and a blind bullock or two, but he would not find a single serviceable cart. Government knowing this made no use of an Impressment Act; they appealed to the zemindars, and the zemindars responded loyally, guaranteeing payment to the unwilling owners of hackeries and promising protection to their families, advancing them money to purchase bullocks and using all those inducements which the zemindar alone can use. The result was that the Government had, in a few days, 7,000 carts collected at Raneegunge. What did the

Calcutta Europeans do? Their loyalty of course cannot be questioned. Did they come forward with their carriage horses for the guns, or their spare hacks for the cavalry: we never heard that they did, although they talked considerably about doing so. The only instance that we recollect of any man's offering his carriage-horses to Government, without payment, was a native zemindar. Every elephant in Bengal was placed gratuitously by the native zemindars at the disposal of the Government, although we know instances in which they were refused by Europeans. None of these men have asked for their elephants again, although they have been gone nearly two years; every one knows how the zemindars came forward to assist the magistrates with men when the Dacca mutineers broke out. The Bengalees are not fighting men, so we could not expect them to clatter about the town of Calcutta for the consideration of a pair of boots, but what was in their power they readily and voluntarily performed. Government never asked them to assist with their horses, but if it had we are quite certain that they would have responded as readily as their British fellow-subjects. To say that they have shared no peril is equally a mistake; they have been treated by the mutineers with little less severity than Europeans. That they insulted the English inhabitants of Calcutta as "a faction" is also a mistake; they, in thei memorial, alluded merely to a faction, and a very insignificant faction as events have shown. We sincerely trust that Mr. Norton may never have any practical knowledge of what a popular rebellion in India is; this is certain, that if he does he will never be able to write about it."—*Indian Field*, 12*th Feb*., 1859.

THE END